What people are saying abou.

Matthew Paul Turner

"Matthew Paul Turner's breezy, warm, conversational style should especially endear him to those under thirty-five. Turner is one of Christianity's fresh voices in the tradition of Rob Bell, Brian McLaren, and Donald Miller."

—*PUBLISHERS WEEKLY*

"Matthew proves that learning the real truth about Jesus can be raw, witty, and redemptive. His broken but magical journey has enriched my own."

—BEBO NORMAN, RECORDING ARTIST

"Matthew Turner is gutsy, raw, and relevant. He has a way of taking a tongue-in-cheek tone with his writing and polishing it with compassion and insight instead of bitterness and angst."

—CAMERON STRANG, PRESIDENT AND CEO OF
RELEVANT MEDIA GROUP

"Matthew Paul Turner is a benchmark on our morning show. The audience has come to love his information, his fun-loving interaction with our team, and the great love of Christian music he brings to our show."

—DANNY CLAYTON, THE FISH RADIO STATION,
MILWAUKEE, WISCONSIN

"Matthew Turner is a groundbreaking voice in music journalism. His refreshing style of sculpting a story is captivating and daring. He leaves behind the trite and digs deep to find the substance in his subjects. Features written by Matthew are on the level of *Rolling Stone*, *Entertainment Weekly*, or *Vanity Fair*. A true leader in his field, I expect Matthew will be a force of change in the future of our industry."

—JACI VELASQUEZ,
AWARD-WINNING RECORDING ARTIST

"Matthew Turner is relevant and understands culture, which enables him to connect to a variety of audiences. Matthew has a comfortable, down-to-earth style and makes a great effort to engage audiences. He has an awesome way of connecting with people and tackling real issues within the music industry."

—J. D. KING, EXECUTIVE DIRECTOR OF LIFEST

"I've worked with Matthew Turner for a number of years and continue to be amazed at his passion for the music industry. On a personal level, I have watched him grow in his walk with the Lord and have seen him stand up for his beliefs—even when it meant risking the approval of others. Matthew is a true disciple."

—JANET CHISMAR,
SENIOR EDITOR OF CROSSWALK.COM

"Matthew is young, energetic, unpretentious, and full of fresh ideas that relate well to the college market."

—REBECCA CHAPPELL, COMMUNICATIONS
PROFESSOR AT ANDERSON UNIVERSITY

HOKEY POKEY

HOKEY

Curious People Finding What Life's All About

POKEY

MATTHEW PAUL TURNER

David C Cook®

transforming lives together

HOKEY POKEY
Published by David C. Cook
4050 Lee Vance View
Colorado Springs, CO 80918 U.S.A.

David C. Cook Distribution Canada
55 Woodslee Avenue, Paris, Ontario, Canada N3L 3E5

David C. Cook U.K., Kingsway Communications
Eastbourne, East Sussex BN23 6NT, England

The Web site addresses recommended throughout this book are offered as a resource
to you. These Web sites are not intended in any way to be or imply an endorsement
on the part of David C. Cook, nor do we vouch for their content.

LCCN 2008920366
ISBN 978-0-7814-4536-8

The Team: Andrea Christian, Amy Kiechlin, Jack Campbell, and Karen Athen
Cover Design: The DesignWorks Group, Tim Green
Interior Design: The DesignWorks Group
Cover Photo: © iStockphoto

Printed in the United States of America
First Edition 2008

1 2 3 4 5 6 7 8 9 10

012508

contents

An adventure is only an inconvenience rightly considered.
An inconvenience is only an adventure wrongly considered.

—G. K. CHESTERTON

acknowledgments

Jessica, thank you for letting me do this crazy job. No matter how many times we've been a few days late on paying the mortgage, you've continued to believe and help me believe that writing is my calling. You have no idea how much your love and encouragement fills my soul and gives me reason to think up sentences and paragraphs. I love you.

A special thanks to my wonderful family for putting up with my stories, my sense of humor, and my love for making pies. Every one of you brings something beautiful to my story. Thank you, Schim family, for welcoming me into your lives with open arms.

A huge thanks to Andrea Christian and everyone else at David C. Cook for believing in what I do. This is such an honor.

Thank you, Tommy (for helping me find a good reason to appreciate Kentucky and for being like a brother—more people should be like you, man; for one, George Michael would still be popular), Rebekah (for managing my life and being an honest friend), Andrea (for being the kind of friend who lets a friend write a crappy first draft), Julie (for your sincerity and for the thirty-some years of friendship), Lee (for making this cover look cooler than I thought it was going to look), Luke (for the miles of really good conversations), Daniel (for being there again and again), Nicci (for answering my gmail chat requests despite being "busy"), Pete (for making me feel like I can go to church again), Julie (for good coffee and better conversation), Lisa (for being such a wonderful hippie green reminder of Jesus), JC (for coming back to life), Wade (for leaving messages on my cell phone), Michael (for sharing a love of Annie Lennox—I'll never tell—Oops!), Dixon (for introducing me to a universally beautiful redemption—I like what I see), Matt (for praying), Chris (for letting me contribute to "the voice" and for being one of the most content and peaceful people I know), and everyone else I know on Facebook.com—consider yourselves poked.

Thank you, God, for all of the above people and for being what life's all about. Help me put my left foot in more often.

author's note

I'm very excited that you've chosen to join me in this conversation about calling. It's my prayer that the stories and ideas within the pages of this book help you reflect on your personal story and what God desires for you. I know that you will probably not relate to every word in this book, and that's okay. Because each of our stories and callings are unique in some ways and alike in others, writing a book about individual purpose has been a difficult challenge for me. While each of us desires to figure out our calling, it's hardly a simple task. Furthermore, how I discover what I'm called to do and how you discover what you're called to do might be very different. But that's okay. That's how God has designed humanity: to think and feel and discover his plan for our lives in a variety of ways. So, to help you navigate your way through this often-cumbersome topic of calling, the book is divided into three different types of content.

1. The Chapters: As with most books, *Hokey Pokey* is divided into chapters. Each one covers a specific topic—one that I believe is important for each of us to think about as we consider what life is all about.

2. Curious People: These sidebars are interviews with people about various topics or stories related to calling. Some of the interviews are focused on a theme, while others cover a small part of a person's story. I did this because I believe it's important for us to understand that calling is not something we arrive at; often, it's an ongoing realization that we discover as we pay attention to what God is doing in our lives

and the world around us. In other words, calling is an ongoing conversation. By reading the thoughts and experiences of others, it's my hope that you will glean a little wisdom and insight into how people from various backgrounds have experienced God and tried to understand his work in the world and how it relates to their overall purpose.

3. My Questions for You: Throughout each chapter, I will ask you a few questions, as if I were interviewing you for this book. These questions are my way of inviting you into the conversation. I hope they will give you the chance to reflect on how God fits into your personal story and perhaps a little insight into what he is doing in your life right now.

Thank you for journeying with me. I hope you enjoy the experience.

Peace,

Matthew Paul Turner

MatthewPaulTurner@gmail.com

curious: an introduction

Not every event in our lives has profound meaning or becomes foundational for the rest of our journey. However, I believe that sometimes (at least, for me) the experiences we have and the people we encounter in this life point to a greater significance than the event itself. More than likely, all of us have had experiences that have played a role in helping us figure out a little about life. I've had several times when a book or a lecture has taught me a life lesson. But I've also learned a lot through conversations, relationships, and yes, conflict. I have come to look at certain events as road signs, leading me, or perhaps guiding me, in a good and healthy direction. All of these moments present opportunities for me to learn, grow, or experience God in my story. Sometimes it's just a small lesson that I learn—something I think about only in that moment. But once in a while an experience points to something that I am supposed to take with me for the long haul. The following conversation, though quite ordinary, has stayed with me for a long time. I'm still in the process of figuring it out.

A Curious Conversation

Despite the fact that I'd only met the man seven minutes ago, I nodded an expressive *yes* when he asked me if he could tell me a story. I didn't agree to chat because I wanted to hear his story; I agreed to it mostly because it's difficult to really say no to that kind of question. Well, I suppose it's possible, but that would require uncomfortable honesty on my part, and when you're sitting in the middle seat on a Southwest flight from BWI to LAX, any additional discomfort could be lethal.

The man I was sitting next to wore tan cargo pants and a light blue Sundance Film Festival T-shirt—something he found at a yard sale in Philly. He sported flip-flops and his hair, although mostly covered up with a baseball cap, looked greasy. Before he began to tell me his story, he shut down his laptop, told one of the flight attendants that she looked like Michelle Pfeiffer (she didn't), and as we jetted down the runway, crossed himself. I assumed that meant he was Catholic, since it seemed to be exactly what my friend Sherry did anytime she boarded a plane, drove a car, or stepped onto a bathroom scale.

Just about the time I had opened to the gossip section of *Us Weekly*—there's nothing like reading about Nicole Richie's thin addiction that makes a five-and-a-half-hour plane ride seem like the good life—the man started talking.

"I've been doing a lot of thinking lately about my life," he said, turning his head my way and looking at me with a passionate glance. "You know, man, I've been doing the kind of thinking where you can almost feel it aging you, and if you didn't know any better, you'd swear that you had become intoxicated with self-absorption. I'm probably thinking too much. Honestly, I think I was born to do that. According to Myers-Briggs, I'm an ENTP. Extrovert. Intuitive. Thinker. Perceiver. That's definitely me in a nutshell; I'm inclined to think God must have shot me up with an extra dose of cognitive capability. Either that or I'm just unstable. I don't know."

He laughed.

"If my father had been the kind of person to use analogies like I do, he probably would have said that I was not only intoxicated by my own thoughts, but that I was in need of therapy."

He laughed again.

"But who am I kidding?" he asked. "Dad didn't believe in therapy of any kind. Everything was black and white with him. He seemed almost incapable of seeing or believing anything that was outside the boundaries of his personal formula for life. As you can probably guess, he and I rarely understood each other, but that was mostly because all too often, I didn't support his formulas. That's always been a fault of mine. I find too much joy in being the devil's advocate, a trait that interestingly enough is quite consistent with an ENTP.

"Unfortunately, Dad died suddenly back in 1997, which is when I tried to stop caring about what he thought of me. But when I really think about it, I'm haunted by the thought that I might actually care more now about his point of view than when he was alive. Of course, that might be partly true because he's not here to argue his point. Dad was right about one thing: I do think far too much about my own existence. To be honest, I probably do it more now than I ever have. I've become consumed by the stories of my past that keep popping up in the back of my head. And you know what's really sad? Oftentimes, it's not the interesting stories that I think about. Nope. The stories that most often consume me tend to be the ones that bother me or leave me feeling empty. And isn't it awful that the stories we are obsessed with end up defining us as individuals, or worse, as sellouts? I'll never forget the time he forced me to take karate."

"Forced you to take karate?" I asked. "Why did he do that?"

"Because my father heard about one of the popular kids from my high school getting his blue belt. His blue belt. That was when Dad looked at me and said, 'I think you should have a blue belt too, Chas!' Of course, I was thinking, *Who frickin' cares about a blue belt?* And, naturally, the guy who ended up being Mr. Blue Belt just so happened to be the person I despised the most at my high school. The kid's name was Jeffrey Smalders. I can still hear my father's voice: 'Doesn't Jeffrey look cool all dressed up in his karate outfit, Son? Gosh, he's really built for a fifteen-year-old, huh?' He said that to me as we walked into the fire department."

"Wait. Fire department?"

"My town didn't have a YMCA or any athletic clubs. My town's fire department was the only place that had a large room that happened to also feature mirrors all along its walls. The mayor allowed karate classes to be held there on Tuesdays and Thursdays."

"Okay, I'm with you. But why were you so against taking karate? I mean, I'm not trying to be unsympathetic, but a lot of kids get forced to learn how to do a roundhouse kick."

"Yeah, that's true. But usually, kids who take karate lessons aren't athletically impaired like I was. And I was pretty much a nerd. And being good at karate wasn't going to make me cool, just like being good at karate doesn't make Steven Seagal cool, and he's lucky enough to have a story line! Besides, I was angry at my father on that first night of karate because I wanted to be home watching Ronald Reagan."

"Ronald Reagan? Why?"

"Oh, I loved everything about the Gipper—his points of view, his speaking voice, his fingernails. I've always said that Reagan should have been better known for his fingernails. They were always manicured and unbitten, a quality I think shows confidence in a person. And do you want to know what speech of his I missed? The one where he told Gorbachev to tear down the Berlin wall. It was only the most historically significant speech of his career. Gosh, that man was brave. And as far as I can tell, he didn't know one lick of karate."

"So I'm guessing you dropped out of karate pretty quickly then, eh?"

"You're getting ahead of me a bit. I'll get there."

"Sorry."

"My father went with me to that first class. You know, he seemed to think that karate was going to be the answer to all of my problems, which, for him, included my joy of reading and my ineptness with all things athletic. 'This night might very well change your life, Chas.' That's what he told me as I stood in my underwear in the fire department's locker room and changed into my uniform. The first hour was pretty boring; I learned some stretching and exercise techniques. I said to Dad, 'Isn't this pretty much yoga?' But then came hour two when I had the pleasure of sitting on the sideline of a blue mat and watching Jeffrey Smalders kick everyone's butt. 'Look at how high Jeffrey can kick, Chas!' my dad said to me while he sat there beside me, gawking at Jeffrey's skill as I imagined the spectators in ancient Rome had as they watched lions pounce on and eat small children. 'Go, Jeff! Kick him, man! Don't let him score another point! Look out! Jeff, get him! Yes! Good job!' That moment was humiliating for me; it was like I was watching what a father-son relationship was supposed to be."

"Wow," I said. "That's hard, man. Did you ever say anything to your father? Did you tell him how that situation made you feel?"

"No! I didn't say anything. Instead of talking, I decided that the best possible retaliation against preppy boy and his little cheerleader friend—my father—would be to try and deny my thoughts, deny being uncoordinated, deny my love for reading, and for once in my life take on my father's need for me to be talented at something physical."

"You felt like you needed to prove something, huh?"

"Yes."

"Oh, I think I know what you were feeling, bro. It was like in that moment you knew what you had to do—who you had to be to earn his approval."

"That's right."

"And since you were only fifteen, it probably felt pretty big to you."

"Like a boulder in my gut."

"And as a way of pursuing your father's respect, I'm sure that somewhere in the back of your mind you were constructing a plot to kick Jeffrey Smalders' butt in karate."

"That was God's plan, bro. As I sat on that hard cold floor and watched Jeffrey spar and my father cheer, whistle, and make verbal love to my archrival, I wanted Jeffrey to feel a little humiliation for once. I would defeat him for every young man in the class of 1989 who had ever felt the sting of being put in their athletic place by Smalders. I would defeat him for every young woman who had ever been lured into lust-filled thoughts by his bulky biceps and his chiseled chest. It was like something had begun to roar inside me. But that was only happening in my imagination; in real life, I was no Captain America. Heck, I wasn't even Ralph Macchio. I was more like Linus."

"Dang, man. So did you go back to karate class the following week?"

"I did."

"To make your statement."

"I guess."

"Did you ever end up getting your blue belt?"

"Nope."

"Green belt?"

"Nope. I got my brown."

"Wow, man. You went one level further than blue. That's awesome. I mean, that's what you wanted to do; so that's cool that you actually accomplished what you set out to do. Most people only dream of getting to that place."

"Yep, I invested every part of my being into karate. I was fueled by the weight inside of me to prove myself to the people of my town—to set myself apart from the ordinary small-town kid. Well, that, and the desire to hear my father cheer for me the way he cheered for Jeffrey. I cared about that, too."

"So, he must have been pleased when you finally got your blue belt and then went on to get your brown, huh?"

"He was happy."

"And did you ever get the chance to spar with Jeffrey?"

"Five times."

"And did you win?"

"I beat him once. The last time we sparred. It was the last match before the two of us graduated, and on that evening I came at him with a vengeance. By that time, Jeffrey was already on his second-level black belt. He was quicker, stronger, and more athletic than me. Still, that night I made everyone at the fire department forget about all of that. It was my night. And believe me, the adrenaline was pumping, man. Coach told me that Jeffrey and I were essentially tied going into the third match. He said I needed to block more and remain balanced. I became extremely focused, and Jeffrey never scored a point during that last match. He was so humiliated by losing that he walked off the mat holding back tears and went right to the locker room. I didn't even get a chance to say anything to him. People were screaming. My father was jumping up and down. He ran onto the mat and hugged me. He told me he was proud of me. It was an interesting night, for sure."

"So you proved yourself!" I said, drinking the last sip of my watered-down cranberry-flavored Sprite. "That must have made you feel amazing. Finally, the good guy beat the crap out of the preppy kid who thought he was better than everyone else."

"Actually, I felt horrible. Sure, I'd won, but when I thought about all that I had given up to get to that spot, I wasn't sure it was worth it."

"You weren't the least bit excited about winning? How is that possible? I mean, you were only a brown belt—the underdog—and you beat Jeffrey, the pompous guy who humiliated everyone? Dude, do you know how many guys would kill for that kind of movie ending? It had to feel a little rewarding. And not to mention, you proved to your father that you had what it takes. Isn't that what life's all about, proving you can do the seemingly impossible? Making everyone you know stop in their tracks and for once notice you? To some extent, that had to feel good!"

"Sure, there was a small part of me that was cheering on the inside," he said, looking at me, and giving me a halfhearted grin. "But it would have been much more impressive for me to have just been myself and not become something I wasn't made to be."

He stopped talking for a moment, and then added, "You know, man, the problem is, most of the time embracing who you were made to be doesn't usually make you popular, and it rarely makes you cool. But you learn that. At least, I did. Even today, I think most of the time I feel just curious enough to be dangerous."

Curious People

Chas is perhaps the most interesting stranger I've ever met on a plane. Vulnerable. Cocky. Obsessive. Emotional. A pilgrim. The thirtysomething had rather insightful observations about his life, from his relationship with his father to his pseudo-knowledge about Myers-Briggs. Sadly, the story he shared was about a man who was still struggling with the fact that he had to become something he wasn't meant to be in order to earn the approval of his father. But that's not what I remember most about Chas. As I walked off the plane, I could not seem to forget his use of the word *curious*. It stuck out for some reason. I kept replaying its meaning and implications over and over again in my head. I thought about how often it gets used in a negative connotation and how ridiculous that is. Think about it: being curious—to be eager or filled with wonder about something—is a beautiful concept. That's especially true in relationship to our calling.

That's why I think we should be curious. I think it should be something we're always pursuing. I think those who experience life are almost always curious people. They're filled with an odd desire to figure out the *why* and *when* and *how* of their story. I'm not only talking about people who are famous, popular, rich, intelligent, or successful. A curious person could be anybody—anybody who's willing to put a little effort into finding out what life is about. I hope this book will share some stories and provide some insights on what it means to pursue the curious path.

My Questions for You

1. Do you ever contemplate how everyday events like meeting strangers on planes or having random conversations at coffeehouses affect you?

2. How have your relationships with your family members empowered or weakened your pursuit of your true passions?

3. Have you ever felt like you have become "unlike yourself" in order to please somebody else?

4. What are you truly curious about?

a curious path

No story is the same to us after a lapse of time; or rather we who read it are no longer the same interpreters.

— GEORGE ELIOT

We Need True Stories

I learned at a very young age the importance of listening to people's stories. My father is a fantastic storyteller. Most of his stories are from his youthful past, growing up on a dairy farm in the 1940s. When I was a child, right before bedtime, Dad would come into my room, sit on my bed, and tell me one of his curious tales as a youngster. His stories had plot. They had mischief. And they always had a moral— one that he wanted me to learn. Now that I am older, I value all of his stories, even the silly ones. I believe they are a part of me in some way. They are my history, my roots, and I hold on to them as I navigate my way through this curious life I've been given. But perhaps the most valuable part of Dad telling me his stories is that he gave me permission to fall asleep imagining and dreaming about my own story. In other words, his stories helped me find my path.

Hearing people's stories encourages us to contemplate our own stories, which often have something to tell us about what our calling is about. And so our stories point to our calling, while our calling sheds some light on the *how* and *what* of our stories. But how do we even begin to find our calling or, if you will, the meaning of our stories? I think one of the ways is by paying attention to our lives and the stories around us, letting them sink in, and hopefully, allowing them to direct us onto a good path.

Believe me, I realize that discovering your calling isn't a simple task. However, it's something that each of us desires to figure out. One of the ways that I personally have connected to my own calling is by carrying with me (figuratively, not literally) a collection of true stories—not just of my own personal experiences, but stories from my family's past, stories that I've read or heard, and stories that have moved me out of my comfort zone. A lot of these stories come from people who have lived a lot longer than I have and who are much wiser.

Life Is Sometimes Unfair

In 1986, when I was only thirteen, my sister Kelley got a job at the local nursing home as an activities coordinator. Though Magnolia Hall was an above-average elder-care facility, Kelley's job consisted of distracting the residents with crafts so they wouldn't realize where they were. Believe it or not, she was successful sometimes. Although the craft projects she organized often did the trick, residents most often forgot their whereabouts when the task at hand involved gambling.

Every Tuesday and Thursday at 2:00 p.m., if a resident wasn't blind, dead, or Baptist, they gathered in the nursing home's cafeteria for an hour's worth of unadulterated, cutthroat bingo. And believe me, those nursing-home folk took their bingo playing very seriously. I was always excited when my sister let me volunteer during bingo hour. Probably more than most adolescents my age, I really enjoyed helping old people do things. For me, helping the elderly was much more fulfilling than helping people who could help themselves. Perhaps I live in some sick kind of reality, but it was always easier for me to understand a Christian's calling to be the hands and feet of God in the world when Kelley assigned my hands to assist Mr. Calkins, the old man who had no arms. I'd often heard my pastor preach against the woes of bingo, but I couldn't understand why when I considered Magnolia Hall's bingo hour. Each week, I saw a glimpse of God in the face of limbless Mr. Calkins. God seemed to show up every time Mr. Calkins borrowed my appendages to place a bingo chip, clap between games, or wipe the snot from his nose.

One afternoon, after bingo was finished, I wheeled Mr. Calkins back to his room. As I pushed him up hallway after hallway, he talked constantly. "Young man, I haven't had my arms for almost five years," he said, his voice chronically raspy. "I lost them because of poor circulation. And do you know, that even though it has been that long, I have never gotten used to not having arms. At least four or five times a day, I reach for something. Or at least I try to reach for something. I can't seem to remember that I ain't got no hands. It's frustrating."

Mr. Calkins' story moved me. In some ways, it still moves me. I felt sorry for him. I didn't understand why life was so unfair. I hated it. I guess at the time, I thought that if you lost something important like your arms, the part of your brain that maneuvers the lost members should go too. But often the opposite is true. Instead of forgetting about what you no longer have, you're usually tempted to think about it more. That's why Mr. Calkins' story, though rather simple, became one I carry around with me. Watching him interact with the other residents despite what he didn't have was inspiring. "You have to look past what you lost or never had to begin with and grab on to the things that you *do* have," he told me. "You can't live in the past, Son."

I don't know about you, but I need to be reminded of what's true sometimes. And sometimes that truth comes from these kinds of ordinary moments—conversations and experiences that remind me of what's important. I learned from Mr. Calkins that I didn't want to focus on what I didn't have or the stuff that I had lost along the way, but instead, on what God had given to me in the here and now.

HOKEY MOMENT

Spend a minute or two thinking of one story that you've heard or experienced that has continued to impact your life.

Does it seem to you that true stories are becoming less and less important to people today? And when I say "true," I don't simply mean something that happened, but rather, stories that lead us to discover truth—perhaps truth about ourselves or about our futures or about our careers. I happen to think that as time goes on, we're hearing fewer and fewer true stories.

I think one of the reasons this has happened is because a lot of us have grown accustomed to most of the stories we hear being doctored up or exaggerated to some degree. In other words, we've let the media and other cultural elements tell us who we should be and how we should live for so long that we often end up feeling like our own stories aren't exciting enough or dramatic enough or sexy enough. So we resist sharing them.

It's quite sad that we as a culture have somewhere along the line become accustomed to hearing and experiencing untrue stories. More than likely, most of us have heard more than a few muted stories on Sunday mornings. We've watched sensationalized ones at the movie theater on Friday nights. And consequently, some of us have exaggerated our own. I will admit that things like special effects, punch lines, and clever storytelling have made some stories exciting and entertaining, but I also think these storytelling techniques have caused a lot of people to stop pursuing their own true stories, often deeming them not important or attractive enough.

I think a lot of us have an addiction to the exaggerated, the processed, the untrue. I believe we're addicted to these kinds of stories the same way we're addicted to caffeine, prescription drugs, and cigarettes. And here's the sad part: I think sometimes those kinds of stories are just as harmful to our health. Our dependence on sensationalism and/or blandness has made the true stories about people—you know, the ones that sometimes have the ability to beckon us out of life's holes with a little hope, seem boring or unmoving to us. Again, I think that's sad, because humans learn by way of narrative. Stories teach us how to live. And if all the stories we hear have been processed to some degree, how are we supposed to truly connect with what our calling might be? How can we find the path toward figuring out life if all we're living in is an unreal world?

The stories of people—realistic ones about regular people living true lives—help us discover our own stories. But what so many of us do not realize is this: The stories we pay attention to end up shaping us. In most instances we become what we believe to be true. Think I'm exaggerating? Look at how many young women are obsessed with their weight and are dieting because they believe "true beauty" is a size two. (It's not, by the way.) And, likewise, consider how many men give their lives over to their jobs because they've grown up in a culture that tells them true success requires them to make $150,000 or more a year. See the danger in untrue stories? They can affect our futures far more than most of us realize.

Calling Is a Path

Hokey Pokey is about getting on a path toward discovering what life is about. Notice that the subtitle to this book does not say "people who have found what life is about." That's because it's not about people who think they've arrived! It's about people who are in the process of discovery. This curious path toward figuring out life is not one that ends. Oh, it's possible to stray off the right path from time to time. And you can get lost. And it's even possible to think you're on the right road when you're not. But don't think of calling as something that you arrive at—because it's not. It's a journey that takes a lifetime. It's a process. And it's important to remember that, no matter who we are or where we are on the path, we are always in process.

I tend to think that most people desire to know what life is about, or at least, have some kind of curiosity about it. For most of us, it's an inner craving, like the need for a good friend or a good conversation or a good foreign beer. I tend to think we want to be in the know about life because we humans are nosey creatures; some of us are hopelessly in love with that feeling of exclusivity that comes when we are in the know about all kinds of stuff, but especially life.

Isn't that why we put so much effort into figuring life out? Those who do, I believe, are brave. I think it takes a healthy dose of curiosity and wonder to lead us onto a journey toward discovering a little meaning in this life. And unfortunately, the path toward doing so isn't easy. Like I said in the introduction, I'm not just talking about the path toward the bigger meaning—everything big and small is somehow sacred—I'm also talking about the kind of meaning that is found in the most ordinary and human parts of life: like in relationships, serving, the jobs we have, and other things that make us smile.

In a nutshell, we crave to know our calling. I think it's a desire that God has given us. Not everyone believes that to be true, but I do. When I read Scripture, I am moved by the stories of men and women who passionately believed they were on earth for a greater purpose. They believed in things that were bigger than themselves. They believed they were called by God to live and do his work. Those of us who follow Jesus carry on that tradition. We believe we are God's children and that we, too, are called to something bigger than what we can see. We are God's hands. We are his feet. And while he is constantly redeeming the story of this world through his Son, Jesus, we are called to join him in that narrative, to look for our places in the story and participate in the work he is doing.

But our beliefs can often make the journey toward knowing the *how* and *why* of this life very complicated. But for some reason, God has given each of us a desire to know something about our meaning, a curiosity that keeps us moving toward figuring life out. And though the road is rocky, the truth is that sometimes the path toward learning the big and small of life's meaning makes us into who we are. In other words, the "process" can teach us something if we allow it to. People who pursue life with an inquisitive spirit sometimes find answers to all or some of those questions: *Why am I here? What am I supposed to do with my life? How can I know if I'm on the right path? Is God involved in my story? Does God even care about me?*

We live in a culture where an awful lot of people want life's answers to come easy and processed so that they're quick to understand. A friend of mine (I'll call him Jason) really enjoys answering people's big questions. No matter what the question—real or rhetorical—he will offer his two cents to anyone about almost any topic. People call him Kramer behind his back because they're convinced that he thinks of himself as the "expert" in almost any situation. And he does always have an easy answer.

"I'm just confused," said the girl, who was a friend of a friend who had joined Jason and me for drinks after work one Tuesday night. I forget exactly what her comment was in reference to, but I think it had to do with her not being married. Or maybe it was about sex. All I remember is that she was confused about something.

"Sometimes I just don't get how I am supposed to *hear* God," she said. "People tell me all the time that I'm supposed to, and I don't believe I've ever heard him."

Most of us around the table just nodded our heads. One person offered, "I think a lot of us are with you there. That's a hard topic for sure."

"Well, have you heard about the four Ps of interacting with God?" asked Jason.

"I don't think so," she said, giving him her complete attention.

"It's easy!" said Jason. "Prepare. Pray. Persist. Promise. I learned this from a pastor back in Jersey. It's just an easy way for me to remember that, when I need answers, I need to get quiet, talk to God, be consistent about talking to God, and then lean on the promises found in his Word. Never fails!"

"And you hear God answer you using this method?"

"Most of the time, and when I don't hear him, I just assume he's telling me no."

Don't you just love when people try to simplify God this way? These kinds of people take something that could potentially be precious, personal, passionate, and maybe a little perplexing and make it seem about as deep as *Sesame Street*. The truth is, the answers to the grandiose questions that we have about life aren't easy to find, and I think this is okay. We shouldn't want the answers to be easy. Easy means we're not willing to get dirty. Easy means we're not embracing life's mysteries. And often, easy means we're living somebody else's story rather than seeking what God would have for us as individuals.

No wonder there are a wealth of people giving easy answers to life's most difficult questions. When I hear some of the perfect four-point solutions that professionals write about in books and project on

PowerPoint displays at seminars, it makes me kind of nauseous. Why am I so distraught by the easy answers? For starters, they are too simple, too processed, too one-size-fits-all. And just as I don't believe we are meant to digest "food" made by Kraft or Campbell's, I don't think we are meant to live within the confines of somebody else's processed path. That's not how we were created, and yet, we still continue to seek the next easy solution because we don't want to do the hard work it takes to lose weight, heal a relationship, or find our dream job. We would rather get what we want in four easy steps. For only $13.99. But we suffer consequences when we embrace such easy *microwavable* answers.

C. S. Lewis said that we are all souls who live and breathe and feel and respond to story. The easy answers may have been sufficient for us at one time in our lives, but they aren't good enough for us right now. Life's big questions do not have easy answers. And that's okay. The easy answers don't consider our passions and desires—the very core of our beings. And we have to consider who we are as individuals when we are talking about something as important as what we were made to do in this world.

My Questions for You

1. Think of someone you have a great deal of respect for in your life. What do you admire about his or her journey that you would like to apply to your own?

2. Have you ever been offered an easy answer to a complicated question? How did this make you feel?

No doubt, calling is a strange topic. When you think about it, there are an awful lot of inconsistencies and uncertainties when it comes to understanding what calling even means. For instance, if I were to ask a hundred people to define their idea of "calling," there's a better-than-average chance that I could get a hundred different answers. Whether our comprehension about calling is limited or flawed or incorrect or perhaps just misconstrued and in process, the topic seems to leave a large portion of the population befuddled.

If that's you, it might help you to know that you're not alone. I think our misunderstandings with calling are kind of normal and maybe even warranted to some degree. Without great amounts of research and experiential study, a person trying to grasp the idea of calling might feel similar to those who started tuning into *Lost* at any point after the second episode. (I don't know about you, but I think the appropriateness of that show's title is astounding.) But I guess that's what makes calling such an interesting topic—one that has throughout time caused people to form a multitude of different opinions about what it entails and how it's discovered. The range of ideas surrounding calling often leaves me perplexed (which quite honestly, isn't some great feat), but that happens mainly because one individual's calling might be another person's way of making ends meet. And, while some people believe they exist *within* their calling, that their entire reason for living is mandated by an invisible and universal force they may call God, others think their calling is something they work toward, that it's something they arrive at or pursue. And, I'm quite sure that some people come up with their own rather imaginative combo of those explanations.

There is a good amount of confusion and fear and uncertainty around calling. It's nobody's fault; I think perplexity is a part of the very nature of the concept. After all, calling is a mystery. For some, the definition of *calling* has to include the question of why we exist, and as you might expect, the answer to that question isn't simple. Quite frankly, even when put in the simplest of terms, each of our answers depends largely on our personal experience and how we interpret that experience.

Some of us like to paint this great mystic picture of personal calling, one that is spiritual and supernatural; others believe the concept of calling is something that we can easily understand—to the point where formulas and surveys can answer any questions we have about the subject. One of the more popular ways of thinking about our calling helms on the idea that calling is about *doing* as opposed to *being*. Made up of an individual's core values, responsibilities, and passions, the more logical thinkers among us suggest that our callings play out in various forms such as employment, family, social standard, and religion. And that's not exactly incorrect thinking.

My personal experience with trying to figure out my calling is that it's sometimes a rather dysfunctional journey, one that ebbs and flows and malfunctions at inappropriate times. And quite honestly, I learned to think of that as a good thing. At least, that's true today. Because that's how we learn, that's how our stories get written—by way of the process or the path. It kind of reminds me of the Chevy Celebrity I owned in college. It was white with blue interior and had a torn off Bush/Quayle '92 sticker on its bumper. Granted, the car almost always *eventually* got me to where I wanted to go, but upon arriving at my destination, those who rode with me promptly exited the car and kissed the ground. Still, I often felt a sense of accomplishment—like I had earned that trip. Sure, some of my friends had arrived twenty or thirty minutes earlier in their BMWs or Geo Trackers, but they arrived without a story to tell. Even though that old car of mine left me feeling frustrated on many occasions, I felt a bit of thrill in never knowing what would take place between where I was and where I was going to end up.

Here's what I've learned: The journey toward figuring out our calling is a little bumpy. But I've also learned that more often than not there's something true to hold on to in just embracing the adventure of the search, in engaging the story of what God is doing or desires to be doing in our lives. No, the story I encounter might not be an epic— but honestly, no matter what John Eldredge might suggest, sometimes epics are overrated (did you see *Alexander*?). But you know, while I may get to experience an epic from time to time, sometimes I just want my life to resemble a limerick, something short but true that makes only a little sense but gives me something to talk and laugh about with friends and strangers. And of course, it should rhyme! The curious path begins with you being willing to focus a little attention on your own story—not in an egocentric manner, but in a way that makes you get honest with yourself so that you will begin to know who you are, what you're good at, and how God fits into your narrative.

I think a lot of times, many of us are too frightened by the adventure that comes with searching, mostly because we're afraid of where it might lead or, scarier still, where it won't. I've certainly had moments in my life when I've resisted the search, choosing rather to sit on my backside in front of the TV and watch somebody else's "adventure," or at least ABC or NBC's overproduced version of somebody's adventure. Many people know what I'm talking about too.

Sadly, sometimes watching thirty minutes of somebody else's woes is a lot easier (and much more entertaining, frankly) than jetting out and experiencing my own.

But people who sit on couches and watch exaggerated versions of other people's stories miss out on hearing, learning, seeing, or experiencing something true for their own story. Not every true experience is good or valid to what's happening in our lives, yet once in a while, we encounter something true that changes our lives or maybe simply changes our day. It's just another mile on the path toward becoming who we're meant to be. Again, it's a process, and finding what life is really all about begins with being brave enough to become curious.

My Questions for You

1. How do you define *calling*?

2. Is the topic of calling confusing for you? If your answer is yes, why? If your answer is no, how do you see your personal calling?

free enough to dance

Freedom is not worth having if it does
not include the freedom to make mistakes.

—GANDHI

A Curious Soul Is Free

You'll see few things more beautiful in this world than a soul that's truly free. I think we're all *called* to be free. I'm not talking about the kind of freedom that comes from living in a democracy, though that's usually a good thing. The freedom that I find truly beautiful is the kind that isn't defined by the expectations of others. It's the kind that allows us to ask questions, be fully human without feeling guilty, and get all-out angry once in a while. It's also the kind that lets you be *you*. But that kind of freedom is difficult to attain, mostly because you can't attain it. It's just a byproduct of living out who we are—who we were created to be.

I believe that God wants us to pursue this journey with passion, but for that to be a possibility, we have to be free. I happen to know what it feels like to live on both sides of freedom. I know very well the freedom I have when I am full of life and joy—the feeling of waking up in the morning to new grace and new possibility. That's the kind of life I desire. And I also know that it's the kind of life God desires for me.

39

But honestly, for much of my life, I haven't lived free. I know all too well what it feels like to live with that nauseating ache that comes from being locked up in fear or codependence or religiosity. Those kinds of things cripple a person's calling, mostly because they only cause one to worry and become preoccupied with things that, for the most part, cannot be controlled. But for me, I've often been so full of fear that I've been scared not to allow other people's ideas about how to live control me, a habit I started to learn when I was a child.

When I was in third grade, a substitute gym teacher—a lady who substituted for nearly every teacher at our school—announced to the class that, because of the rain, we weren't going to be able to go outside. "But I think we should play some games! How about the 'hokey pokey'?" she asked. I'd never heard of the hokey pokey; I suppose because I lived in a hole or, as some called it, fundamentalism. Sure, most kids could perform the hokey-pokey song and dance in their sleep by the time they reached third grade, but it sounded dirty to me. You see, my church and school didn't allow frivolous activities such as dancing, so I couldn't remember a time I had ever felt free enough to "shake it all about." In my class of fifteen eight-year-olds, none of us were free enough to do that.

"Everyone get in a circle!" yelled Ms. Hartman, who was obese and often smelled like her Pekinese. "Let's do the hokey pokey!"

Despite Ms. Hartman being an awful excuse for a gym teacher— the poor soul wore muumuus—everyone loved her because she was kind and let us break some of the school's less important rules when other teachers weren't around. She was quite the rebel. And in those days getting the chance to chew gum often made us feel as revolutionary as Martin Luther King Jr.

"What's the hokey pokey?" asked one of the kids, looking around the room with an expression that said, *I don't think we should do it.*

"You don't know the hokey pokey?" asked Ms. Hartman, throwing up her arms in disbelief, and whispering something naughty under her breath, "Are you kidding me?"

"Is it a game?" asked another kid.

"Well, some might call it a game, but I think it's more like a song and dance."

"We're not allowed to dance," I said, not wanting to be caught leading any one of my brothers and sisters in the Lord astray. "Dancing is sexual!"

"Sexual? That's nonsense!" said Ms. Hartman. "You can do this dance! I'm sure even God does the hokey pokey once in a while. Get into a circle!"

We followed Ms. Hartman's instructions and formed a circle—although most of us were quite nervous that lightning was going to strike because a teacher had just suggested that God might actually move his body to the beats of music not made by angels with harps. As she began talking us through each of the actions to the hokey pokey, it became clear that to our beloved overweight substitute teacher, putting your left foot in was much more than mere child's play. To her, this fun little song and dance seemed to be more like a manifesto than a song—one that was a testament to how she tried to live her life and wanted us to live ours. When one of the kids was only halfheartedly doing the motions, fearful that his or her parents would balk at such rebellion, Ms. Hartman went ballistic. "No. No. No! You do it like this!" she said, and then she'd jump in front of us and demonstrate how to do the move. But you could tell that, in addition to teaching us how to dance the hokey pokey, there was a part of her that was also teaching us how to live life. "You have to put your *all* into it; don't halfheartedly do anything," she encouraged. "And don't fear looking foolish! Who cares what other people think? You have to be free!" Ms. Hartman didn't seem to care that everything jiggled uncontrollably when she put her body in and took her body out. It didn't faze her that a couple of kids laughed. She also didn't care that teachers would once in a while talk behind her back. She wanted us to taste a little freedom, even if it was just for a thirty-five-minute gym class. And it was only the *hokey pokey*. As fearful as I was to dance, as afraid as I was of getting into trouble, by the end of the thirty-five minutes, I thought gym class was over much too quickly. Even the smallest amount of freedom feels good enough to breathe a little life into your bones.

Are You Free?

Truthfully, probably only a few people are fully free. I think I've met one or two elderly people who are darn close, but freedom is something that happens to an individual over time, and each of us learns it or experiences it in ways that are unique to our situation. Pursuing your calling requires you to also be on a path toward becoming free. Think about your life for a moment: What keeps you locked up and unable to be yourself—the person God made you to be? Is it relationships? Fear? Depression? Anxiety? Is it the fear to ask questions? There are so many ideas and realities that encage us and keep us from living. Sometimes the cages we live in are a state of mind, a way of thinking that limits the potential God has for us. Other times it's how we live our lives that cripples our ability to engage life with any kind of passion.

You see, on one side of freedom, there is something—call it grace—that pushes us to live and experience life the way we were meant to; and then, on the other side, is a cage that limits us, in some cases paralyzing us inside the walls of our own thinking, our mistakes, our fears of failing, or our feelings of hopelessness. And often, we feel like we've hit a dead end.

My Questions for You

1. How do you see freedom being an important commodity in the journey toward finding your calling?

2. Do you believe that you're on a path toward freedom?

3. What kinds of things keep you from being free?

Free Your Christian Mind

Probably like a lot of Americans born in the latter part of the twentieth century, I've always had moderately high expectations for my personal story. To be honest, I haven't met too many people who wake up in the morning and think to themselves, *I was born to be a loser*. Oh, I'm sure these people exist, but I've not met too many of them. And let's face it; even if you do wake up thinking these kinds of thoughts, in today's culture even a "loser" can find reasonable success using YouTube and MySpace.

But like most normal kids who were raised in small-town America in the '70s and '80s, I didn't want to be a loser. I went through moments where I believed that God wasn't on my side, that he was going to make the road to "success"—whatever that looked like—an arduous journey for me. More than a few times during my life I've believed that God spends his free time in heaven thinking of ways to thwart my plans, or going out of his way to make whatever is going on in my life much more difficult. As you might imagine, that hasn't always been too helpful. Throughout my life, I've found that much of the time I didn't view God as very supportive or loving or, at times, even present. The way people talked about God to me made him seem small-minded or harsh. But that happened because I allowed other people's comments and beliefs to dictate my opinions about God and his plans for my life. And so I started to believe that he was a part of the problem rather than part of any kind of solution.

I realize now that my perception of God plays such an integral part in how I live my story and how I view the calling on my own life. How I view God can either make me free or leave me crippled in chains. I believe that's true for each of us. Do we see him as Savior? Father? A distant watchmaker? The thoughts and feelings and experiences that make up "God" in our lives can either push us to explore, create, and live freely, or they can encage and limit our potential. And because we Christians so often think we have God all figured out, we do a lot of encaging and limiting instead of freeing people to create and explore and live. I think what I find so frustrating is that, at times, we think we are so sure about how God thinks and feels that we have the audacity to package him up with shrink-wrap and sell him at merchandise tables during break times at conferences and concerts.

HOKEY MOMENT

How do you view God? Is he a helper? Is he the big meanie who limits your potential? Or is he your lover and sustainer? Do you think of him as someone who dreams right along with you? Take a moment and contemplate your perspective of God and how that affects your ability to live freely.

When I was a senior in college, just beginning to look for my own personal spot in the world, someone I used to call a friend tricked me into attending one of those monstrous Christian conferences. At twenty-one, I was pretty much an idiot who believed I had it all figured out. For starters, I was convinced that politics solved things, believed that God was like a kinder but less patient Judge Judy, and thought I would become cool if I was a vegetarian. Unfortunately, I never had enough willpower to stop eating meat—sub sandwiches were my weakness. Willpower, or the lack thereof, has always been a problem for me. Maybe that's why my friends believed I needed to attend a Christian conference—to fix what ailed me. I think they were under the impression that this conference they were dragging me to would help me become some kind of apostle Paul–defined superhuman.

Now, if you're not familiar with monstrous Christian conferences, you might picture them as large pep rallies for God. They're actually events where you gather with other Christians in order to learn how the Christian life is *supposed* to be lived. Most of the time you learn this from people who have in some way seemingly *perfected* the Christian way of living (or as is sometimes the case, *created* the Christian way of living). The conference I attended was held in Nashville, the city where I went to college at Belmont University, and the conference's theme was "Finding God's Purpose for Your Life." And really, what twenty-one-year-old doesn't want to do that?

So, to that end, for two-and-a-half days I sat in a large room listening to Christian pros wax pretty much nonphilosophically about a various number of topics, including: "How pornography kills brain cells," "God's strategy for life," "It all begins with worship," and "God's way of dating." During the presentation for that last topic—dating—a twenty-two-year-old man stood up and talked about the hardships of being single, and then at the end of his presentation, introduced the audience to his fiancée. And the crowd gave him a standing ovation as if a twenty-two-year-old *engaged* man had some idea about the hardships of being single.

As I listened to the various jocks-turned-Christian-pros talk about their individual expertise like they were anchors on ESPN, I couldn't help but wonder to myself, *Are these guys anywhere closer to figuring life out than I am?* At the time, I doubted it, but I was scared having that opinion might make me unpopular or worse, a heretic. And when you're Christian and rather insecure, there are few things scarier than being dubbed unpopular and a heretic. To my surprise though, some people I talked to were brave enough to question what they were hearing. They asked questions … lots of questions. Sometimes the questions were good ones, thoughts I certainly had from time to time. And sometimes the questions were humorous. While one of the speakers talked about the dangers of online porn, my friend leaned over and whispered, "You know very well that guy still masturbates. You know it! So, why is he making us feel crappy for not having it all together?" My friend had a good point, although not a popular one, but it was good. And it did make me laugh (although fearfully).

A year ago a Christian college near Chicago asked me to speak to their students. It was that university's spiritual-life week: three days set aside for the students and faculty to focus their attention on God things. Each night I gave a talk, which mostly consisted of me telling stories about *my* life. I don't aim to be narcissistic when I give lectures, but as you have probably noticed, I am not a preacher or a theologian. I consider myself to be a storyteller (with opinions—lots of them). So whenever I am asked to come and chat with people in a live setting, I retell stories, mostly personal ones about my experiences with God, how I maneuver my way through the madness of Christian culture, and what I believe are the most important ideals of this life we live. Like with many speaking opportunities, when I visited this university, I met a number of students who could relate to my personal narrative, including Zack, a twenty-one-year-old senior. The shy religion major approached me after the final evening.

"I have to be honest with you, man; I didn't like you the first night," he said to me right off the bat, which caught me off guard for a moment. When the first thing out of someone's mouth is a criticism, it's difficult to know how to respond. However, I didn't say anything; I just listened to him.

"I went home after your first talk, thinking to myself, *What was that guy's point? He just told stories.* I've never heard an author just share stories before. Usually, they share advice or biblical theory or something else I've heard a thousand times."

Zack's voice cracked a little.

"For some reason, even though I didn't care for the first talk, I had to come back last night and again tonight. I didn't really want to. But I kind of felt led to come back. And I'm so glad I did. The last two nights were somewhat enlightening for me. You and I have pretty much identical stories. Both of us were raised in superconservative churches. Our fathers were both deacons. We went to Christian high schools. I pretty much lived your life except I'm not in the same place ten years later." He laughed.

"But I have to ask you: How did you break the cycle? How did you get free?"

He just looked at me.

"Cycle? What do you mean?" I asked, wanting to be sure I knew what he was asking.

"Well, you seem to have gotten away from depending on what other people expected you to think about God to figuring things out. How did you do it? How did you overcome the fear? Do your parents hate you now? I can't do it. And I need to! I want to. I feel like I'm suffocating. I don't even know what I believe anymore. About God. About Christianity. About anything of real meaning, really. And it's not like you can just express stuff like that around here. Professors aren't much for hearing about a student's doubt or big-picture questions. They just want to make sure you have the Four Spiritual Laws memorized, which seem to be the answer to everything."

I knew exactly what he was talking about. I knew his struggle all too well. He didn't feel like he had the freedom to ask questions, to doubt, to be frustrated about his way of life. Like so many of those from the twenty-first century who have asked evangelicalism into their hearts, Zack had gotten to a place where he felt duped. For almost twenty years he'd invested his heart and soul into a way of living that made a lot of big promises. He was promised that God's will would be clear. He was promised that his life would eventually fall into place if he learned how to obey. The processes that he followed included lots of things practical Christians do: praying three times a day, reading his Bible, working up a good amount of honesty with an accountability partner. But even though he followed all of the rules, he still felt lost. I know a lot of people whose stories are similar to Zack's. Toward the end of our conversation, Zack said to me, "I'm not having a faith crisis here; it feels more like a life crisis."

And he was right; it was a life crisis—one that happens to a lot of us because we don't know how to be free. Because faith in God is an element of our lives that is rooted in the deepest parts of our psyche, the questions and thoughts and doubts that filled his brain did not merely represent a breakdown of belief. The obstacles that Zack talked to me about had become a life disorder. Everything he was about was affected in some fashion: relationships, his pursuit of a career, his emotional stability, and also his ability to work past guilt. And according to Zack, the answers from all of those Christian professionals who seemed to believe they owned the copyright on truth didn't work. Not for him.

I didn't have any foolproof answers for Zack, so I just offered this: "Zack, get free, bro. God is not the kind of God who is going to zap us if we do something wrong. He loves you. He wants you to be certain of that. No matter what you do or where you do it, he loves you! Live and make decisions with that confidence in mind." I didn't give him a process by which to learn about God's love. I didn't give him one of my books. And you know what? Even if I had thought that all of the answers to his questions existed, I knew enough about timing not to offer them. So I just gave him a reminder: God loves you. He wants you to be free. The same is true for all of us. Like so many people I know, Zack seemed to be searching for the freedom to *be*.

Jasper Collins knows that feeling. She and I met by accident one time when I was in Portland, Oregon, many years ago. The evangelically raised woman was a friend of a friend, and when that mutual friend of ours was married, we became kindred spirits for the weekend. "Most Christians are locked up with their to-do lists, Matthew!" she exclaimed during one of our lengthier conversations. "That was me only a few years ago. And sometimes, I still have to battle the chains in order to live a little life and be true to my story. You know what I mean?"

Jasper wasn't born in the states; her parents were missionaries to New Guinea. She spent her first seven years in what she calls "a tribal setting." "Seriously, Matthew," she said, looking at her husband with a knowing grin, "I was raised in an area that looked a lot like where *The Swiss Family Robinson* was filmed."

"I *loved* that movie!" I said.

"When my family moved back to the states, going back to an American church was awful. Before then, I'd only experienced worshipping God on the beach in my bathing suit. And sometimes for us kids, the bathing suit was optional. Once back in the states, all of that freedom we experienced was squelched by a different culture—America's version of Christianity—one that we didn't understand."

Jasper's family fell knee-deep into fundamentalism, the kind that requires women to never show any skin, lean on the men for advice and leadership, and opt out of their dreams to instead go and do whatever their husbands wanted them to do.

"It was a Christian cult of sorts," she said, laughing. "But you know, it wasn't funny. I grew up believing that I was somehow less important than my brothers, that what God had made me to do wasn't nearly as important."

"You've obviously overcome some of that," I said, noticing that she wasn't dressed like a woman from the nineteenth century.

"Yes, I have," she laughed.

"Sounds like there's a story," I said.

"I wish I could say it was an eloquent one, but it's not. When I graduated from high school, I knew one thing: I wanted to recapture the God-experiences that I vaguely remembered having as a six-year-old in New Guinea. My faith wasn't dependent on a nicely furnished building; in fact, it wasn't about a place at all. Back then there weren't any 'rules' for engaging God. But in the states, not only are there rules for engaging God, there are checklists to help you know whether or not you're a *true* follower, and there are people who will come in and correct you if one of the points on the checklist becomes an ongoing, unmet issue. Though the 'process' makes it simple for those doing the *checking*, I don't believe we humans were made to engage God in this manner. There has to be a freedom of expression in our pursuit of God, you know? God didn't make us to relate to him all in the same way. I was made a certain way for a purpose."

"And so, how did you eventually get some of that back?"

"Well, in college I actually tried the culture's way of doing things. I became a partier, experimented with some recreational drugs, and basically just became like a lot of the other girls who were only interested in living for themselves. And while that way of life is fun, it didn't bring me peace. So I continued to struggle to find where I fit in.

"For my college graduation, Mom and Dad, who have been so supportive of me through all the various struggles that I've encountered in life, gave me plane tickets for me and a friend of mine to go to New Guinea. In the card Dad wrote, 'I want you to go back to where your faith began and rediscover that little girl again.' I cried for an hour over how thoughtful that was. Seven weeks later my friend Jill and I were traveling to the place where I was born."

"Did that help you?" I asked. "Was it the experience you needed to put you on a healthier and, um, freer path?"

"Do you want to know what I did? I found the little village where I lived, which was no easy feat. But we eventually did find it. We stayed overnight at this little hotel that was just a little shady. And the next morning, I told Jill that I needed some time alone on the beach. I walked onto an empty beach at 5:30 in the morning. The sun was just beginning to peek up over the water. I stood there and wept and prayed and worshipped God. As I stood there, feeling freer than I had felt in a long time, I knelt down onto a blanket and just meditated and remembered and healed. When I finally walked back to the hotel, I really, truly believed that I was on a path toward being free, a path that I had longed to find since I was a child. Do you have any idea what that kind of freedom feels like?"

"Yeah, I do," I said. "I think I do anyway."

My Questions for You

1. How has your past affected your ability to live life today? Do you feel freer? Or do you feel as though there are chains around your neck?

2. Do you truly believe that God desires you to live freely?

3. Have you ever tried to live somebody else's spiritual story? In other words, have you looked at another person's life and tried to emulate their path because of how God was working in their life?

Are You Free Enough to Question God?

The following conversation took place on a Sunday evening in St. Louis. I don't reveal the names of those involved—the *who* doesn't really matter—but I think this dialogue between two friends says a lot about having the freedom to *believe* and also the freedom to *not believe*. Faith requires both, I think.

MAN #1: *(Standing)* Dude, what's wrong with you? You act like something's bothering you. What's on that beautiful mind of yours?

MAN #2: *(Sitting on a bench, smoking)* I don't know, man. Nothing? Everything? Eh, I'll be all right. My head is just full of questions. *Big* questions. Small questions. Uh, to be honest, questions that scare me. I'm not even sure I should say them out loud.

MAN #1: What kind of questions are you talking about? Life stuff?

MAN #2: *(Looking at his friend)* I don't *get* God. Not like I did when I was a kid, or two months ago.

MAN #1: Oh. I'm sorry to hear that, man.

MAN #2: But my problem is that it's beginning to weigh me down some. You know, I've never been at the place where I am right now. I've never *not* understood how God fits into my life. And now, everything feels upside down. But here I am; thirty years old and just beginning to *not* understand all the stuff that we're supposed to believe in, man. It's starting to not make any sense.

MAN #1: What "stuff" are you talking about, man? Just say it. Stop being so cryptic. You're not making much sense.

MAN #2: Well, this isn't simple for me.

MAN #1: I'm your friend; it's okay to talk with me about it. I'm not going to judge you.

MAN #2: I'm talking about the stuff that you and I have been told is absolutely true since we were kids. You know, the basics—the stuff that a good many preachers consider to be the foundations for faith. For instance, did Adam and Eve really exist? Or have we been lied to all of our lives?

MAN #1: Well, for what it's worth, I believe they did. But I've gone through moments when I've doubted that.

MAN #2: But, dude, why do you believe they existed? Is it because you *truly* believe it happened, or because you're too scared not to believe it? Do you have faith, or do you have fear in God?

MAN #1: I don't know how to answer, man. I guess …

MAN #2: *(Interrupting his friend)* Did you know that there are other stories from that same time period that are almost identical to the story of Adam and Eve? And, *please*, I'm just wondering if you know that. I mean, I'm not saying that I don't believe God exists. But think about it: What if—and I'm just saying *what if*—the Adam and Eve story was simply a way for God-fearers to tell their kids about how the world began? Still an *inspired* story, but not actual events, you know? It would kind of make sense.

MAN #1: I guess I just *choose* to believe it's true.

MAN #2: *(Rolling his eyes)* But does it make sense to you?

MAN #1: *(Looking at his friend)* I don't think it has to make sense to me. I think it's the way God chose to tell his story, and that's his prerogative.

MAN #2: Dude, I'm not trying to start something here. I don't want to argue. I can't help that I have these questions. Do you think I want to doubt these things? Because, believe me, I don't. I wish I could say with all authority that everything in the Bible was absolutely true and that I could say I believed everything that *whatever* Bible church says is true. I have believed it. But at this moment in time, I can't.

MAN #1: I'm not mad. I guess I just don't know what to say. But I guess I know that nothing I can say would be all that helpful.

MAN #2: Can I ask you a question: Have you ever thought about what it would have been like to have been born a Philistine?

MAN #1: Not really.

MAN #2: Well, it's my assessment that a Philistine's life would have pretty much just sucked. And it wasn't necessarily because they had a choice on whether or not their life sucked; it just did. Simply because he or she was *born* a Philistine, they were already hated by

God. Is that fair? Think about it: Is that fair? Because both of us have been raised in churches that call that reality *just. The justice of God!* How is that even remotely just?

MAN #1: I don't know. But again, I guess I don't feel like I have to know all of the answers to believe that there's a God who loves me. Do you believe that God loves you?

MAN #2: Dude, are you listening to anything that I'm saying? I'm not questioning God. I'm not questioning Jesus. I still believe in God.

MAN #1: Well, you are questioning him to some extent, at least, the way that he decided to tell his story.

MAN #2: I knew that I should have kept my questions to myself.

MAN #1: I'm not mad at you, bro. All of us have questions about our faith. Believe me, I have questions. I realize that following Jesus isn't simple, bro, and that I don't understand everything the Bible talks about. And I certainly don't believe it all fits together like one gigantic puzzle. Some of it doesn't make much sense.

MAN #2: But haven't we always been taught that in order for us to have *true* faith in God, that there is a list of things that do have to fit together? I mean, am I right?

MAN #1: Yeah, you're right to a large degree. But, man, it doesn't have to make sense. Faith isn't about making sense. If it were about that, it wouldn't be faith! I think they would have called it science or something. Unfortunately, those who do most of the preaching make the Christian life sound like it's this well-defined system that all you have to do is plug yourself into. But we can't spend our lives fighting the "powers" of American evangelicalism, because that will just lead to bitterness and anger, man …

MAN #2: And that's just it; I'm angry. I'm angry at those who taught me that I have to think a particular way in order to consider myself Christian, that I don't have any freedom to wonder and dream and doubt.

MAN #1: But you do have that freedom. God doesn't disown you because of your humanity.

MAN #2: But let me ask you this: Can I be a Christian without believing that the Word of God is 100 percent infallible?

MAN #1: Of course you can.

MAN #2: *You think?*

MAN #1: In the end, bro, I think it comes down to knowing this: Jesus is the Redeemer. Every human's life is wholeheartedly hope-dependent upon his death and resurrection. And I believe Jesus' power to redeem is much bigger than we can ever imagine. And it's not our place to decide who gets redeemed and who doesn't. But our lives, the things we do every day, should constantly be challenged by the teachings of Jesus. I don't think he minds if we doubt, but I do think he cares whether we love our neighbor, stay humble, and do the things he asked of us.

MAN #2: I guess that would depend on who my neighbor is …

MAN #1: *(Laughs)* I hear you there. But, man, please. Don't be afraid to ask questions, no matter how big they are. Just ask them with humility and not with anger. We're on a journey. And the answers we find don't come easy.

Wiggling Free

The cages we experience differ. For Zack, it was a thick religious past that seemed to limit his potential, but for others it might be success, selfishness, capitalism, drugs, sexual promiscuity, family, relationships, or other realities that shape who we are, shape our stories, and shape our understanding of life. For some of us, it's all of the above. Only you can know what's happening inside your head.

I have learned through experience that how we live life affects our ability to live our calling. Consider codependence. If a person is unhealthily codependent on another individual or on a job or on a church, that will normally translate into not being free enough to make decisions on his or her own. A codependent person is too preoccupied with what somebody thinks about them or too preoccupied with controlling a situation that they can't even begin to experience their own calling. How can someone do what God wants him or her to do when he or she is mentally and emotionally consumed with somebody else's life? That's a cage. And as long as you're codependent, it's almost impossible for you to be on a curious path—one that will lead you toward encountering God, experiencing a full life, and doing what you were made to do. The same is true for any area of your life that is not on a path toward becoming free.

Life is about learning how to wiggle free—at least enough to begin experiencing what God has made *you* to experience. Some might wish there were some kind of magic formula that could make us free, and while that might seem like a nice thing, I think there's something that we can learn in the process of becoming free. I have learned so much about myself on the road toward freedom. Sometimes that road has been a process of prayer and meditation. Sometimes it has been a journey through counseling and/or medication. Other times a taste of freedom comes from an experience.

When I was twenty-three, I was in Pennsylvania at a world music festival on a blistering hot June day. For that reason, I took off my shirt and scrunched it up into a ball. I kept using it to wipe up the beads of sweat that were dripping down my forehead. The air was thick with the smell of humidity, beer, cotton candy, and hot asphalt. And while those smells don't seem like they would be all that appealing, the combination of smells brought back some of my best memories.

I was standing on a friend's Mexican blanket—you know, the kind that was probably bought during a 1990 family vacation to the Caribbean and advertised as handmade in Cancun or Mexico City, but eventually you find out that the tag reads "Made in Bangladesh." Even though I was simply one among the thousands of other people who were gathered on that Pennsylvanian hillside, I kind of felt like I was all alone in my own personal universe. My eyes were closed, and I was reveling in the sweet sounds of a band that I assumed had probably gotten high somewhere backstage when no one was looking. But that didn't matter. Even the most evangelical of us has learned that people who are high certainly make some ridiculously cool music at times. That band's guitar rhythms were contagious. The horns were almost uplifting. And the congas seemed to be talking to me, whispering what felt like temptations in my ear.

And no, I wasn't high, though the music might have made me feel that way.

For as long as I live, I'll never forget June 26, 1996; that's when I danced for the first time. And even though I'm quite sure that the movements I did that day—some kind of back-and-forth two-step with my hands clapping—can't really be called dancing, for the first time my feet, hands, and body moved freely to the infectious beats that filled my ears, my head, and eventually, my soul. As weird as this might seem, I believe I evolved that day. I changed into something new. As my physical self became free enough to move without hesitation, without fear, the freedom I experienced made me better suited for my natural environment: the distinct culture and time where God intentionally placed me so that I would grow, serve, and become a small fragment of holiness. That's what a little taste of "free" can do for people—allow them to not only know their self-worth but also to feel it.

I've learned on more than one occasion that the freedom to experience your calling sometimes just comes by getting out and living life—by just putting your left foot in. So don't complicate the journey. Just go ahead and live: Ask the questions. Make that decision without your friend's approval. Be okay not being in a relationship. Don't believe everything your pastor tells you. Be okay with the fact that your job doesn't pay much. Stop feeling guilty about yesterday's mistake. Find joy in the fact that you're the only one of your friends who believes in God. And if you want to, dance. Go somewhere and get your groove on. Be free. Be you.

HOKEY MOMENT

Take a moment and ask God to help you see
the areas of your life where you need to be free.

it's not about you

There is one body and one Spirit,
just as you are called in one hope of your calling;

one Lord, one faith, one baptism;

one God and Father of all, who is above all,
and through all, and in you all.

—PAUL THE APOSTLE

Calling Might Be Bigger Than You Imagined

One of the misconceptions about calling that I believe a lot of us have is what parts of our lives it encompasses. When I was a college student, I assumed *calling* was simply a new-agey term to discuss the relationship between what I was passionate about and what I would eventually get paid to do. Back then I strived for the best possible option—to somehow find a way to make my living doing what I was passionate about. But since then, I've been awakened to a grander perspective of calling—one that weaves itself in and out of every aspect of our lives. Over the years I've learned that I am not alone in thinking that calling is bigger than we might think. It's not simply what we do for a living; our calling, in fact, is actually how we live every aspect of our lives.

A few years ago I was sitting at Le Peep, a small midscale diner that's only a mile or two from where I live. Fifteen minutes after I arrived, a wealthy businesswoman from another table wearing an expensive fluorescent orange scarf looked up and gasped, "Oh, my gosh, there's Amy Grant! Look! Do you see her?"

The lady was staring right at me when she spoke, but because her voice was loud—like an announcer—I believe she might have been talking to the entire diner. Once she looked around the restaurant to see who was paying attention, she leaned back in her chair to make it easier for people to look out the window. I'm not sure why she did this. Perhaps she thought I didn't believe her, or perhaps she was just being kind and wanted to make sure that everyone in the restaurant got a glimpse of one of Nashville's most loved celebrities.

When Amy walked into Le Peep, the only entourage she had behind her was her youngest child, Corrina. I don't believe she had any idea that the entire room was watching her as she sat down at my table. In fact, I was definitely far more aware of how envied I was to be having breakfast with Amy Grant than Amy was of the room's nosey reaction. Every time I've been in the same room as Amy—which has been only a handful of times—I've noticed that she seems rather oblivious to the attention she receives. And from my vantage point, it's not false humility that makes her seemingly clueless to the stares and whispers that happen around her. One of her friends said to me once, "Um, yeah, that's just the way she is—one of the most polite and kind people in the world."

"Sorry I'm a little late," she said, smiling. "The traffic was crazy this morning. Let me just get Corrina settled and then we can talk. She'll just sit here and color."

The first time I met Amy, I was supposed to be protecting her from overzealous fans like myself. She was performing at a charity event at Belmont, and I was one of the students chosen for artist security. But instead of working to ensure her safety from the thousands of rabid fans, I walked up to her and told her how much I loved her. Amy was gracious, giving me several minutes of her undivided attention. A few moments after the encounter one of the event's organizers grabbed my arm and then yelled into my ear. "If I see you talking to another artist, I'll have you kicked out of this program so fast, your head will spin."

We had no real agenda that morning. Amy and I had become acquaintances during my stint as editor of *CCM*, a magazine that profiles the artists who make Christian music. I'd interviewed her for a cover story in 2002. During that conversation, I asked Amy about the topic of calling.

"You know, I've never really thought of what I do as a calling," she said. "I know I'm not the best singer or the best songwriter; I tend to believe I was just in the right place at the right time. There are thousands of people more talented than me. But for some reason, I've been able to do this for the last twenty-five years."

At the time, her response shocked me. I thought, *If somebody like Amy Grant, a woman whose career in music and ministry was seemingly dropped into her lap at age sixteen, doesn't believe she was* called *to be a singer/songwriter, then where in the world does that leave the rest of us?* But perhaps I had a tainted perspective on the idea of calling. During that interview, I didn't press her on the topic, but when we sat down for breakfast, I asked her about it.

"When I interviewed you a couple of years ago, you said

something that I found very interesting. And for my own personal well-being, I wanted to ask you about it. You said that you didn't think you were called to do what you do. To be honest, that kind of shocked me; how is it possible that you don't believe you were called to this career?"

She looked down for a moment and then back at me.

"I just think to say that you're called to do something is a really big statement. I feel like my 'calling' is the same as everybody's; it's to be a good mom to my children, a good daughter, a good citizen, a good steward of the opportunities that I've been fortunate enough to experience. I think *living* life is everybody's calling. For me to say that I was called to play music or called to be an entertainer or whatever has never been all that comfortable. I think that puts words in God's mouth. Am I called to *something*? Yes, but I don't believe that just because someone experiences a certain amount of success in one area suggests that we were called to that career—at least, not like Abraham or Moses were called by God. Calling to me is more ongoing than that; it's so much more than simply 'what people get paid to do.'"

"Do you think that any of the experiences you've encountered with your career fall into that 'calling' that all of us have on our lives?" I asked.

"I think that's true for everyone. A person's calling doesn't necessarily change with occupation. It might grow or become more intense because of what somebody does for a living, but it doesn't change. I think our calling is to love and serve people in whatever experiences we find ourselves encountering. That's the greatest calling we can be a part of."

My Questions for You

1. Have you thought of calling and career as the exact same idea?

2. Does it surprise you that someone as "successful" as Amy Grant doesn't view music as her calling?

3. How do you live out your calling in your life today?

Does God Call Us to Something Specific?

The following story is *almost* entirely true:

A few years ago I was in Kentucky at a Christian music festival where I ran into Kirk Cameron. Yes, *that* Kirk Cameron. Though in 1988 Kirk Cameron was "it," I was hardly starstruck by the encounter. I mean, how could I be? This was the same guy who starred as "Buck" in those awful *Left Behind* movies. But I wanted to talk to him because I kind of felt sorry for him; the former kid star was sitting all alone in one of the corners of the backstage tents eating a bag of Cheetos and drinking a Diet Coke. I'd never thought about it before, but I realized that it must kind of stink to know that while people might care about what and who you are now, they still liked you better when you were playing a rebellious teenager with a good-boy smile. But all that didn't stop me from telling him that my fourteen-year-old neighbor had a big crush on Mike Seaver. Yet, according to Kirk, that was never his true calling.

"So you've started preaching, huh?" I asked. I had seen him on

TBN so I already knew the answer to that question, but I wasn't ready to say good-bye just yet.

"Yes, I have," he said in a tone that sounded exactly like Mike Seaver. "I've been doing it for a few years now."

"So, I gotta ask; are you anything like Mike? I mean, how much of you went into that character?"

Awkward silence.

"You know, that's a part of my life that I don't really enjoy talking about anymore. Please don't take offense to that, but I'm really into what I'm doing now."

He smiled.

"Do you have any desire to act again?"

"Nah, I really enjoy talking to people about God; I feel like this is one of the things I was made for. God designed me this way."

Awkward silence.

"Well, it's really good meeting you! Maybe I'll catch you again after your next talk."

Each of us has a story. Each of our stories is precious to God. I believe that with all of my heart. I don't claim to understand how God makes choices about who will do one thing and who will do another. I have quite a few questions about how it all works. I'd love to know if the dreams that we have come from him or if they come from the culture we live in. And if they sometimes come from him, how can we know the difference? Seriously, it can all become rather laborious.

There are lots of theories about whether or not each of us is called to a specific career. I have friends who say they were born to be car salesmen—that schmoozing is in their blood. Other friends of mine believe they were born to be poets, but would starve to death if they ever tried to make a living with their talent. So they work at Wal-Mart or as copy editors. While some Christians have come to the conclusion that God has one ideal career path for people (most believe that is based on one's talent), others think we're all called to live by the same values and that "what we do with our lives" is up to us. I tend to believe that it's a combination of the two, and that the combo is rather complicated.

The Bible itself can make things confusing. All throughout Scripture there are stories about men and women being called to very specific things. I love these stories. They are inspiring. They give me the freedom to dream and imagine how God would want my life to be. They give me a lot of hope when I'm in a place where I feel lost or down. Some of the biblical stories contain miraculous events that were meant for that one individual. Some of them are high on drama. All of them are very much stories about humans following God the best way they know how.

The stories are endless: Abraham was called to be the father of the Jewish people. God chose Moses to lead Israel out of captivity. Esther was called to help her people. David was called by God to become king. And the list goes on. It's no wonder so many of us believe that we, too, have been called to do something miraculous during our time on earth.

But I've found some commonality among God's "specific" callings. Some of God's callings within Scripture were huge, lifelong, and life-changing pursuits that required men and women to act on faith—to listen to God when logic seemed to ask them to do something different. However, for every unique calling in

Scripture, there are mentions of other people—millions of them—
who didn't seem to have the same type of calling on their lives. I
mean, while God might have told King Solomon that he would be
the richest man in all of the world, does that mean he also called
those who worked for him to be his helpers, his slaves, his lovers, or
his wives? Consider Moses. Though Moses was called to do
something specific—lead God's people out of Egypt—what were
the million or so Israelites who followed him into the wilderness
called to do? Seemingly, they were each called to play a role in
helping their community survive; each of them had different
talents, but their "roles" in this existence was very much the same.
And I don't believe that makes the million followers any less
important than Moses; however, their callings were very different. It
was communal.

I have always found it difficult to assume that God has designed
the perfect job for each of us. To me, it just seems strange that God
would make each of us for a very specific "career" in this life. I
realize he gives us talents, things that we're good at, and things that
we're not good at. And, I'm not necessarily suggesting that he
doesn't have plans for each of us; I'm just not sure he creates each of
us for a role that no one else can fill. I think it's a little more
complicated than simply thinking to ourselves, *I am born for
something very specific and great*.

Today's culture has turned "calling"—as it relates to career—
into something that is very individualistic. It's about *you* getting to
where you want to be in thirty years. It's about *you* saving up for
retirement. It's about *you* standing on your own two feet. And I
think if we're honest with ourselves, that's how most of us look at it.

Interestingly enough, the Bible doesn't support such a theory. Whenever someone was called to a "specific something," it was almost always for the good of the community, an entire people, not just the individual.

Sometimes I wonder if we haven't skewed God's story to fit our own. I know that's been true for me at times. Most of you reading this book have been raised in the same culture as me: the United States. I'm inclined to think that some of my basic belief systems about calling, career, and what I'm born to do have come from the way I was raised in America. It's very American to grow up believing we are meant to live a particular life, do a particular thing, and make a particular amount of money. Of course, we can't help the culture we have been raised in. That wasn't our choice.

However, we do have the ability to assess our personal stories and open our eyes to both the good and maybe the not-so-good effects of being raised American and how that has affected our perspective on calling. Think about this: What are the ramifications of being raised in a culture that puts a great deal of attention on fame, media, celebrity, wealth, notoriety, and other things that God doesn't seem to necessarily value? Now, I'm sure that some of us have been able to escape the effects of a society that seems to only want to empower the almighty "me." But many of us haven't been able to escape it. For years we've been measuring our lives against the standards that we have been subjected to. Too many of us are quick to compare our own lives with what our culture says is good and true instead of aligning our lives with what God says is good and true, which, when all is said and done, is our true calling.

HOKEY MOMENT

Reflect on how the culture you live in has affected
your perspective of calling. Ask God to teach you
what *he* says about your calling.

When I was twenty-eight, I realized that, when it came to my
personal understanding about calling and career—you know, thinking
the two words were synonyms—I was little more than an American
twentysomething who didn't have a clue. That's when I began
wondering, *Why in the world am I here?* or *What is my story really
supposed to be about?* More than likely, you've probably asked yourself
both of those questions a few times.

My boss at the coffeehouse I worked at also happened to be a lay
psychologist, which always made "business meetings" a little like group
therapy. Actually, business meetings *were* very much like therapy.
Oftentimes right in the middle of talking about "numbers," we would
cry, hug, and pour out all of our feelings like we were in a church
small group or AA. *My name is Matthew, and I run a Christian
ministry.* In addition to making sure I was doing my job correctly, my
boss also had a habit of doing regular screenings of my psyche.
Sometimes I got one-on-one therapy with my boss. I can't tell you
how many times we sat around and talked about our lives instead of
getting any work accomplished. It was mostly *my* life we talked about,
and I usually learned something worth taking home with me. None
of it helped me keep the coffeehouse open, but it did make me feel
good about myself.

"Bill, can I tell you something?" I asked my boss who was looking at me so intently I wondered whether or not he already knew what I was going to say.

"Oh, come on, you know you can talk to me about anything, Matthew," said Bill in a very kind manner, almost laughing.

"Yeah, I know," I said. "But it feels polite to ask."

"Whatever," he said. "What's on your mind?"

"Well, to be honest, I'm feeling kind of depressed lately," I said.

"Oh, I know you have been depressed, Matthew; it's written all over your face."

His comment caught me off guard.

"It is?" I asked.

"Yes. You might as well just spill it, my friend," he said, putting his hand on his chin and gently rubbing his soul patch. "Talk to me about it."

"Well, I don't know how to begin; it just seems that at certain times I think my life is rather pointless," I said. "I mean, look at me; I'm twenty-eight, and I manage a coffeehouse! Not that that's a bad thing, but it's not necessarily what I believed I would be doing two years shy of thirty. You know? I just don't think I'm doing anything purposeful. Does that make sense?"

"Well," he said, cocking his head to one side and cracking his neck, "how are you measuring your purpose, Matthew?"

"What do you mean?"

"What do you think is purposeful? I mean, how do you know that your own life is meaningless if you don't know what is purposeful?"

I sat there and thought for a second.

"I'm not sure; you're talking to a guy who gets up every day and comes to a place where I make a lot of coffee and lattes, book some cool Christian bands, and don't usually get home until late at night after the last show. I know that's not really a life, but is that purpose?"

"To some people that's a lot of purpose, Matthew!" he said, smiling. "Do you know how many people would love to be getting paid to do what you do?"

"I guess so. But it's not like we're all that successful here. We can't make this place break even. If we didn't have a very wealthy owner who gave us a lot of money each month, we wouldn't still be here. And furthermore, I guess I feel like I was made for more than just coffee and booking gigs, you know?"

"Like what?" he asked.

"I don't know."

"Well, what would be your idea of *more*? And please, don't hold back. Pretend you're not talking to the guy who could fire you and send you back to Chestertown, Maryland."

Again, he laughed, and then added, "You go ahead and feel free to say anything at all."

I just stared at him. I didn't know what to say.

"No, go ahead, Matthew; if you could do anything in the world—something that would make you feel like you had some purpose—what would it be?"

"Like I said, I don't know what that would be. I think there are lots of things that could potentially make me feel like I had a little more purpose. I enjoy people, so working in some capacity with people does make me feel good."

"Okay, but you're missing the point. Purpose is not just about your career, Matthew. Purpose is tied into every aspect of your life. So don't mistakenly believe that your job or what you do professionally will eventually be what makes you happy. It might help, but on average, what we do for a living doesn't make us happy. Sure, it might play a small role in what makes us happy, but it can't be everything."

"But this place is my life. I mean, do you know the last time I had a day off? Or even felt the freedom to take a day off?"

"But that can be fixed, Matthew!"

"Okay, Bill, can you just give me some kind of direction on how I should think about all of this?" I asked. "I mean, I don't really want you to think for me, but I'm tired of being down about my life. At the end of the day, there's a part of me that just wants to have a wife and a family. I want to feel like the work I do has value. You know, like helping people. I want to be able to afford a home. It doesn't have to be a big home, just something I can call my own. I'd like to someday be well-off financially, maybe even rich …"

"Okay, stop right there! I love you too much to sit here and listen to this. And besides, I am already very well aware what the American dream is, Matthew," he said, rolling his eyes. "I don't need to be reminded of what almost every other person in this country would *love* to have. Now, before you get angry with me, hear me out."

I was glad he said that because I was indeed getting angry with him. But I kept listening.

"This is why I was asking you about how you measured your purpose. If you ask me, I think you're trying to figure out life by way of comparing your life to the standard that the culture of this country has said is the 'right' way to live. Now, don't get me wrong; it might be the *nice* way to live and the *practical* way to live, but is it the *right* way? At least, is it the *right* way to live for you?"

"Well …"

"No, let me finish, Matthew. It sounds to me like you want to live the comfortable life. And sure, sometimes comfortable is nice. But is it *right*? Do you know that some of the happiest people I know have very uncomfortable and socially 'unacceptable' employment? It's true. They're not rich people. But they're happy people. I happen to believe that a part of their happiness is because their lives aren't built around what they do nine to five. You know what I mean? They find their meaning in all of what life has to offer. Their calling isn't the sum of how they spend forty hours a week; it's all of their life combined that brings them joy. Not all of us are born to do things that make us rich and famous and comfortable. In fact, sometimes I wonder if *comfortable* isn't about as ungodly as you can get. I happen to think that some of us were simply born to live the lives that are in front of us, and sadly, the American way has slowly taken the joy out of that kind of lifestyle."

"But I don't understand. I mean, are you saying that I should stay here? Or are you saying that I should wait on God?"

"Matthew, I am saying that you're correct about being called to something bigger than Jammin' Java. That's true for all of us. But that calling might not be what serves as your paycheck. It might not have anything to do with your job. Remember that. Purpose is found in the sum of life. You're called to live life! Are you doing that?"

Sometimes Bill's therapy was really nice. Before meeting him, I'd never known anyone to be so free about speaking into somebody's life and telling him or her exactly what he or she didn't want to hear. But that was my boss Bill. Sometimes he was a bit like an annoying father who wandered into your personal life without asking—didn't watch

where he was stepping, and sometimes he looked under the bed to see
if you had any porn hidden underneath the mattress. But despite Bill's
lack of boundaries, every time we chatted about the deeper stuff of life,
I learned something.

I continue to learn.

Curious People: Aaron Carriere

Aaron is a friend who worked with me on the publicity of one of my
books. Last year, he left his paying gig and ventured out on his own
to pursue what he believes he was made to do. Or something like
that.

MATTHEW: Aaron, when you got out of college, did you
feel called to something? And if so, what was that?

AARON: I entered college in search of stability and money,
and sort of shed the dreams I had in favor of security. I
graduated with a public-relations degree and knew all
along that PR wasn't my passion, but I had to go into it to
land my first "real job."

MATTHEW: Did you feel writing was your "calling"? In
other words, do you believe you were born to write?

AARON: Honestly, I think defining "my calling" is still a
work in progress and always will be. Writing is part of it,
but I believe my calling—as well as that of many others—

is simply "to create," to create in response to our Creator. God revealed this phrase to me about three years ago, and it really cast a vision for what "my calling" really may be. This has taken on many forms, and I haven't arrived anywhere yet. God has laid a vision for it, but we have to work through it and pursue it in tangible ways, which takes on a number of forms. It's a lifelong process.

MATTHEW: Do you think that humanity has been called to create? Or is this something that is specific to your life?

AARON: Yes, I think everyone is called to create in response to being created. It takes different forms, of course. I think we often miss our "calling" when we pursue ends for ourselves. I've learned this the hard way, and God has humbled me in order to realign my thinking that I'm in charge.

MATTHEW: A year or so ago, you took a huge leap of faith and started your own "creative business." What have you learned from that journey?

AARON: There have been a number of lessons; it has been a life-changing experience. Honestly, the most important lesson I've learned is that God is in control, that he is my provider, and that he wants me to partner with him in this life. The danger of pride and the necessity of humility has also been a tough lesson.

MATTHEW: How have you seen God provide?

AARON: I've seen God provide out of desperation and brokenness. I ran completely out of money in the winter—my car was broken down, I couldn't pay my bills, and I had little work on the horizon. One night at church, two friends gave me a white envelope full of money they had received from their wedding and told me that God had prompted them to give it to me. I completely broke down. It was unbelievable grace. There have been a number of stories like that in the past year.

MATTHEW: That's awesome, man. How are you "creating" today?

AARON: To me, there's an interesting correlation between money and faithfulness. I'm not one to preach any sort of prosperity gospel, but I've seen God provide out of faithfulness, and I've seen God take away from disobedience. For me, "creating" has taken on many forms, mainly through video, writing, and music—both in the professional world and also recreational. It's a progression and all interrelated, and I think we're in a place where we're exploring different avenues to find out where we best fit in and how we can make an impact.

MATTHEW: What did you learn about God last summer when you trekked across Europe?

AARON: Europe was all about God's beauty, no question

about it. I'm wired with a certain edge of cynicism, and God really began to challenge me on that by revealing the beauty in his creation and through a diverse group of people.

MATTHEW: Do you hear from God, and if so, how does that happen for you?

AARON: A pastor of mine gave a great sermon on Samuel, where he says, "Speak, Lord, for your servant is listening." I believe that God is always speaking to us, but unless we take the posture of listening and asking like Samuel, we often miss it. I've had experiences where God has clearly revealed himself to me, with three very specific, intense incidences of silence and prayer that cast a vision for what I should be doing. I've also chosen at times to not pursue God's voice, to push him away, and isolate myself, where I believe I can handle it on my own, and those times of disobedience have been the most miserable times of my life. I've always struggled with prayer, but I've found over the past six months how important prayer is, and how important it is to be still and listen with no agenda. God is working in our everyday lives, and we need to listen and watch and pay attention to the things that are going on around us. To borrow a phrase, "There's no separation between the secular and the sacred." God wants all of us, all the time, but we have to be available and make space for that. God also reveals things to us through other people. I think living in community has been so important to develop a clearer awareness of gifts and abilities. A friend challenged me a few years ago to start playing guitar at church—I was terrified at the time, but slowly God quieted the nerves and really opened up an opportunity to serve the church in that capacity. Other people see qualities in us that we often don't recognize. If we develop relationships that are attentive and responsive to each other and centered on our growth, we can help bring out the natural gifts and abilities of our friends, which will impact the entire community and beyond.

I've been a full-time writer for nearly five years. Since then, I've managed to somehow get my name on more than fifteen books. But when I sat down in front of my laptop to begin writing my first book back in 2003, the first thing I did was wonder what in the world I was doing. It's true. I was way out of my league. I didn't know how to write a book. In fact, I still wonder from time to time: *How on earth did I get here?* I wonder that because I scored that first deal, not because I was a great writer, but because I knew somebody who could make it happen. Yep, I knew the right person and so the right place was easy to find. It was most definitely surreal writing the words "*The Christian Culture Survival Guide* by Matthew Paul Turner" at the top of a blank Microsoft Word document. I smiled a lot when I first wrote those words, but then I laughed out loud, mostly because I had no idea what I was going to type next.

Writing didn't come natural to me. To be honest, I kind of tripped into it. I hate telling unpublished writers how I got published because it's not very helpful to them. It's almost embarrassing, because unlike most writers, when I was growing up, I never once wanted to be a writer. I didn't wake up in the morning dreaming about becoming someone like C. S. Lewis or Walt Whitman. In fact, even though I wrote lyrics to songs and a few poems every now and then, my high school English teacher would probably have suggested that I not consider anything involving the construction of sentences as a viable career option.

Like any good grandmother, my Mammom was convinced that I was born to do something amazing. Now, she wasn't a prophet (at least, not to my knowledge), but on several occasions I do remember my grandmother telling me that God had something very special in store for me. Back then, I believed her. Sadly, for quite some time a part of me hoped that meant I was going to one day end up being the Michael Jackson of Christian music. I know—that right there should probably make you close this book now and never read another one of my books. No, it's true; I can't tell you how many times I've thanked God that a few less fortunate people ended up *beating it* prior to me getting a chance. Whew. That's grace. But despite not getting my chance to play the part of God's King of Pop, I've wondered a few times whether or not my gig as a writer was that "something special" Mammom always talked about.

Once, a college student asked me in front of a room full of people if I thought writing was my calling. As soon as the words popped out of his mouth, a large amount of fear began making its way into the gut of my soul. "Um, well," I said, while I searched for a better cliché than the one I was about to say, "I can't really say it's exactly my calling." I looked around the room at all of the faces that stared back at me. "And I know this is going to sound like a big Christian cliché,"

I said, hoping that context would redeem me, "but I have to believe, when I consider the manner in which I fell into this career, that writing is definitely a part of God's calling for my life. I would never have thought that writing would be my career. It doesn't make sense for me. But for some reason God saw fit to use the little bit of talent that I have been able to develop as a writer. Does that answer your question?"

"Yeah, it does, but can I ask one more?" he said, looking at me.

"Sure, go ahead."

"Is that scary to say? Do you know what I mean? Is it scary for you to say, 'It's God's calling for your life' out loud?"

"Yeah, it's scary," I said. "Because I know *me*. And because I know me, I know very well that I'm not anything special; that's for sure. And I've made a million mistakes. I've fought pride. I've had times when I believed that I was a good writer. I've put words in God's mouth. But I still know that somehow—and I don't know how, really—God planned for me to do what I do. I think all of us have *something* that God has designed us for. But I think that always involves the good of a community. It's not just about what *we* want to do. And let me tell you, the journey toward your own calling doesn't come easy. Writing has been the most difficult journey for me. I love it more than anything, but it's not easy. Sometimes I think the only reason I am still able to continue doing it is because God has graced me with a wife who is my biggest cheerleader, and even when we're right in the middle of a very hard spot, she always reminds me that I'm not living *my* calling, that I'm living out God's. And that what I do is not for me."

My Questions for You

1. Do you feel like you were made for a specific role in the world?

2. How has your journey supported your belief?

searching for a burning bush

*When I'm praying, when I'm truly praying, I'm not
thinking, I'm not speaking, I'm shutting up, so perhaps
if God has something to say I can hear it.*

—MADELEINE L'ENGLE

The Relationship of Faith and Calling

Most of us think that life would be simpler if only God would
make himself and/or his will absolutely clear to us. I think a lot of
us are convinced that if God still used his "fiery cloud method" of
leading people through deserts and up onto mountains, maybe we
wouldn't feel so much anxiety about what we should be doing with
our lives. Maybe we wouldn't feel lost most of the time. Maybe our
faith would be stronger, or at least healthier, just knowing he was
around. Honestly, it does seem like it would be much simpler if
God acted a little more like a psychic-help line—one that we could
call and instantly know what decision we should make regarding
this or that.

I'm not sure there is another area of life where we crave to hear

85

from God more than when we're trying to figure out our personal calling. We don't like to be left out of God's plan or seemingly so. We want his voice to be clear and loud and consistent. Why? Because when we're figuring out what we should be doing with our lives, most of us, as I just mentioned, believe it's much easier having God lead us around like a dog on a leash than it is to walk by faith. It's our calling to walk by faith, and it takes faith to live out our calling.

When I was volunteering as a youth group leader, I led a teenage guys Bible study that met once a week. The question that those young men asked the most (other than one about masturbation), was this: *Does God speak?* It was a valid question, one that I had pondered on more than one occasion, especially when I was younger.

When I was a kid, my father took me to our postman Mr. Bolden's house to see his sanctuary of birds. The word *sanctuary* probably makes it sound more grandiose than it was; it was actually just a very large birdcage. As a hobby, Mr. Bolden kept all kinds of birds—thirty or so different kinds—locked up behind chicken wire to show his affection for the feathered creatures. I always liked the "birdman," as I called him, mainly because he had two of the largest peacocks I had ever seen.

Among the peacocks, pigeons, waterfowl, and other strange birds, my favorite was a small duck that normally could only be found in South America; it was blue and black and brown and had the most beautifully painted wings, but according to Mr. Bolden it was not created to ever fly. "It just waddles and swims and poops," he told my father and me as we gawked at it from outside its cage. After watching that duck sit on its butt for what seemed like a very long time (in reality, it was only five or six minutes), I told my father that I believed God had called me to help that bird learn how to use its wings to fly. I was a strange six-year-old, but to me it seemed like a tragedy to have feathers and not be able to use them.

"How do you plan to do that?" my father asked as we drove away from our local bird world. I didn't know how I was going to help birds learn how to fly; I had just thought up the idea only moments before I'd spoken and hadn't yet made up any kind of flight strategy. When I was a kid, despite loving my father, I was still pretty much convinced that the only thing grown-ups were good at was getting in the way of a kid's good idea. They seemed to be tall fat people who enjoyed ruining good ideas by always asking how it was going to get done.

"Maybe God will help me know how to teach that little duck how to fly," I replied.

Like most who were raised in a home that celebrated some kind of Christian understanding, it was easy for me to believe that God could (and would) help me do anything. I believed that with all of my heart. Of course, when I was eight, I didn't have any contact with the poor people in Africa or know anything about the child slaves in India and hadn't heard anything about the persecutions in China, so I didn't see any reason why God wouldn't/couldn't give me the ability to help Mr. Bolden's flightless birds. Today, I might consider it wasteful to ask God to help South American birds when there are babies who are starving in China. But back then, I believed that some kind of "inside" voice was always calling me to do something profound, pointless, or impossible. I was always listening and believed with all of my heart that God would do something miraculous.

Curious People: Joshua Longbrake

I met Joshua after he wrote an opinion piece for RelevantMagazine.com; he came through Nashville on his way to seminary last summer, and I interviewed him about his trip to Europe and how being overseas helped him listen for God's voice.

MATTHEW: Joshua, you recently graduated from college and then you traveled throughout Europe; what kept you from jumping right into the workforce?

JOSHUA: I didn't want to grow up. (Laughs) Nah, that's not true. At least, it's not entirely true. You know, the truth is, I grew up in a very rural part of Indiana. My town has like thirteen people in it. Okay, so it's not quite that small, but it's small. And so, after college, I wanted to experience a little bit of the world before I ventured into whatever I was going to end up doing professionally. So I trekked around nearly twenty different countries for a few months. It was an amazing experience. I'd do it again in a heartbeat.

MATTHEW: What did you enjoy most about Europe?

JOSHUA: The European culture is comprised of such a diverse grouping of people. I love that about other cultures—they are so free to express themselves in the ways that come natural to them. I also loved the architecture. There's just something awe-inspiring about engaging God with thirteenth-century art around you. It makes you feel very close to God. It's just an amazing and worshipful environment.

MATTHEW: What did you learn about God during that time?

JOSHUA: I learned how to listen to God. Listening for God's voice is sometimes so difficult for me. But whenever I am in another country, I don't have nearly as much noise around me. You know what I mean? Now, that might be due to the lack of cell service or the fact that I'm on a vacation-like experience, but I also believe it's because I'm able to hear God more distinctly when I'm not subject to all of the "stuff" that interrupts an American's day. It's just so sad that we're always so busy. There are so many messages that are constantly being thrown at us from all directions. I mean, how often do we get a chance to seek God's voice for more than a few moments at a time. Even in some of the busiest European cities, the culture is still much simpler than ours and has fewer distractions. And for me, when there are fewer distractions I am able to hear God. His voice doesn't seem as small when I'm out of my element.

MATTHEW: When you got there, did you ask God to reveal anything in particular?

JOSHUA: Yes, actually, I did. I wanted God to lead me into great conversations with people. I wanted to talk to anybody he wanted me to talk to. That's really all I asked of him. Every morning I woke up and asked God to lead me to those who he wanted me to meet, and to those I could be light to. Because of my prayers, I ended up meeting so many people who taught me about God. I know God answers prayers, but sometimes it's just amazing to see it so clearly right in front of your face. It really strengthens your faith.

MATTHEW: Why do you think God would care about introducing you to random people across Europe?

JOSHUA: That's a good question. When I was a young teenager, my mother died from cancer. Through experiencing that difficult journey, I learned that God truly does care about the small details of our lives. I watched as he filled in the voids that I felt. What Jesus said was true: If God cares for the lilies enough to dress them up so beautifully, then how much more does he care for people? When you've experienced the big and small graces of God, I think it's only natural to want to extend those graces to those he puts in front of us. I think that's why I went to Europe—to be an extension of God's love and grace to the people I met.

My Questions for You

1. Has God ever spoken to you? Was it audible? An inside voice? Through a friend?

2. How has your perspective of God speaking changed since you were a child?

3. Do you believe that God still gives people signs and/or wonders to help them navigate through life?

Is It Really As Easy As Opening Your Ears?

Before writing this book, I didn't know Jansen Spray, an ordinary New York State native who lives in Pennsylvania. When I petitioned those who frequent my Web site for personal stories regarding the topic of this book—calling—Jansen sent me an e-mail, telling me that he was interested in sharing his story. "If you think it's good enough," he wrote. A few days later, we chatted by phone.

Several years ago, the twenty-six-year-old left college a year early because he heard a voice telling him to move to the inner city of Philadelphia to feed and care for kids whose lives were overrun by poverty, violence, drugs, and hopelessness. "The kids I come in contact with have pretty much nothing to call their own," he said. "And even though I didn't feel like I had a lot to offer them, I came to Philadelphia with an open mind, willing to do just about anything to help. I just listened to what I heard."

He says the "voice" was very emphatic about what he was supposed to do. "I heard it loud and clear! It said, 'I want you to move to Philadelphia, and when you get there, I will show you what to do,'" said Jansen. And according to the young missionary, a title he struggles to call himself, the "voice" even argued back at him when his first inclination was to ignore it.

"It wouldn't take no for an answer!"

Obviously, Jansen either put up a pretty pathetic fight or he just gave in, and with only a few of his life's belongings, moved to the slums of Philly.

"And you're convinced that you were called to move, right?" I asked.

"*Absolutely*," he said, with just a hint of cockiness in his voice, "I believe that with all of my heart!"

"Okay, and please don't take this the wrong way, but was there a phone call that you received? I mean, did this voice have your cell phone number?"

"*No!*" he said, laughing.

"Oh, I'm just asking," I said; "it makes for a better story. Did you know someone in Philadelphia who got you interested in moving?"

"No, it was nothing like that. I didn't know anyone in Philly."

"Are you a part of a cult?"

"No, I'm not involved in any cult."

"You sure?"

"Yes."

"And you believe the voice you heard was God's, right?"

"Yes, with all of my heart."

When I visited Jansen's blog and saw a picture of him, I was sort of surprised at how ordinary he looked. I guess I sort of expected him to look like an evangelist who shopped at places like Sears and always carried around a Bible or something written by Max Lucado. And while there's nothing wrong with shopping at Sears or reading Max Lucado books, that was just what I expected. But actually, Jansen looks like a pretty normal person. He doesn't speak funny or use words that only the evangelical elite can understand. He doesn't talk in a sing-songy tone that some Christians do when they believe they're just a little holier than the rest of us or because they're the lead singer in a Christian praise band. The young, dark-complexioned lover of all-things involving skateboarding actually seemed to be a rather likable guy. Yeah, he heard voices, but still, very likable.

However, let's be honest here. I'm not sure Jansen is normal. I mean, is it normal for a twenty-one-year-old young man to trade the comfort of his home in upstate New York and also a soon-to-be-had degree in engineering for life lived in a two-room dumpy apartment that only has one amenity: running water? I don't think that's normal! Call me crazy, but I've been walking around in Christian circles since I was four years old, and so, I know a good number of Christian people. Most of them are very nice people, but the majority of them live in homes with central air-conditioning and give to "needs" from afar without having to get their hands dirty. Most of them have cable and iPods and only touch dirty kids when their children are playing in the mud. I don't know too many who feel *called* to purposefully live among the poor.

Jansen's excuse for doing it? A voice made him do it. Jansen comes from a pretty well-to-do family in upper New York State. He's been following God for most of his life, but he said with a sad tone, "It wasn't until I was in college that I took my faith seriously. [While there] I started honing in on God's Word, working toward becoming one with the small community of believers there. The twenty or so of us sought after God together. And many of us heard God speaking during this time."

Not everybody liked the idea that he was listening to "voices." His parents, despite being longtime Christians—his father is a deacon—threw a holy fit when he told them about his plans. "You would have thought I had just told them I was addicted to drugs or something. Their mouths dropped open and then they pretty much told me I was crazy for even considering this path," he said, laughing. "To some extent, they're correct; I am crazy. But the way I see it, life is about being crazy once in a while. If you're choosing to follow Jesus in this life, I think *crazy* is a requirement."

"Hmm. I'll have to come back to that last statement in a moment," I said, "but first, I want to know: Did your parents' reaction surprise you?"

"No, not at all! I knew they weren't going to be excited about this," he said, "but they didn't hear the voice I heard. It wasn't their calling, so I expected them to not be happy about it. Mom and Dad interact with God differently than I do; they don't believe that he speaks to us unless it's through Scripture or a pastor or Michael W. Smith."

But in defense of Jansen's parents, they are certainly not alone in that kind of thinking. To non-Christians and even to some Christians, it sounds whacky that a person would suggest he or she hears a voice telling them to go places or not go places, pursue things and not pursue other things. While some non-Christians might believe Jansen is whacked because he is convinced that a voice led him to Philly, certain Christians seem to think God's voice has gone away because God said all that he needed to when the Bible was written.

But to those who hear and listen to this so-called voice, it's a reality that is ever-present in the life of humanity, kind of like Paris Hilton's "career." They don't always understand it, but they hear it and feel it. Oprah even mentions the "voice" from time to time. Once, on her show, she told her audience, "If you know your innermost gut is telling you something, I believe that's God speaking to us. You need to follow it!"

"But Jansen," I said, "is it really a voice you hear? In other words, was it audible?"

"No, it wasn't an audible voice. I like to explain it as an inner leading," he said. "It's this feeling in my heart and mind that urges me to be still or move or do whatever really."

"Do you always hear it?"

"No, not always. And there are some days when I wish I didn't hear it."

"Are you hearing it now?" I asked.

He laughed, but I wasn't able to get him to answer that question.

My Questions for You

1. In what ways does God speak to you?

2. If you believed God was giving you a specific message, would you listen?

3. Is there any part of Jansen's story that makes you skeptical?

Curious People: Judy West

After meeting Judy West in Atlanta, I knew that I wanted to talk to this pastor about her personal story. She's practical, yet she's also very open to embracing the mystery of God. In this interview, I chatted with Judy about her interaction with God:

MATTHEW: As a pastor, what do you believe to be true about hearing God in the twenty-first century?

JUDY: I believe he speaks all the time. Now, I'm not a super-emotional kind of woman, so it's not like I sense him around every corner. But God has never stopped communicating with people.

MATTHEW: You are a former atheist. How has that affected your perspective about God?

JUDY: Oh, I definitely think it has had an impact on my faith, especially when I think about how I came to know God. I didn't have one of those experiences where one day I didn't believe and the next I did. I'm a rather practical and realistic person. I'm not going to believe something just for the sake of believing it. I asked a thousand or more questions and eased into knowing God. If I didn't understand something, I went to Greg (her pastor) and I said, "I don't get this; what is God supposed to be telling me with this?" And after I got his answer, I went back and researched it for myself. But I didn't believe anything until I was darn ready to.

MATTHEW: When you and I first met, you made a very interesting comment to me; you told me that you joined the National Organization of Women (NOW) because it was the only place where you felt welcomed. Talk to me about that.

JUDY: I was living in Pittsburgh at the time and I was married. My husband was in med school, and I was lonely. Yes, a very lonely atheist. (Laughs) NOW ended up being a place where I found friends—people who *got* me and wanted to have me around. I just felt at home there because they accepted me for me. And I hadn't ever experienced that before.

MATTHEW: Before you became a Christian, did you see God show up in your story?

JUDY: I'm not sure this was God, but there was one time when I was in college that I saw a feature on *20/20* about a church where people could wear jeans! I know, *so controversial!* But I remember seeing that piece and telling God, "If I find a church like that, I would go there." Eventually, my husband and I moved here to Missouri.

MATTHEW: Do you think God has created us to experience him in different ways? And if so, what always connects you to God?

JUDY: I think God has made each of us unique in the way we connect to him. Some people connect with him by doing only churchy things. Some people connect with him when there's lots of noise or when they're with a large group of people. I connect with him through nature. That's when I see his glory and creativity. I'm a runner. Long distances. I usually have a running partner who will go running with me. But sometimes, when I've had a rough day or when I'm about to kill my kids or when I know that God wants to spend time with me, I will go running alone. That's when I pray. That's when I listen for God. I think each of us should be willing to engage life and God the way he has made us to. Sometimes churches don't allow us to do that!

My "Hearing" Experience

When I was seven, while my mother was out shopping, I heard a voice say to me, "Your mom is going to buy you a stuffed groundhog plush toy and give it to you when she gets home!" It was almost February and for some odd reason when I was a kid I loved Groundhog Day (not the movie, the *day*), so the mere thought that God told me that Mom was buying me a stuffed rodent got me very excited. While I waited for Mom to come home, I prayed to God, thanking him for letting me in on Mom's secret. When I heard Mom's car pulling into the driveway, I ran out to greet her.

"Where's my stuffed animal?" I said in a tone that wasn't demanding, just full of excitement.

"Stuffed animal?" my mom asked.

"God told me that you were going to bring me home a stuffed groundhog!" I said, wanting to believe that Mom was simply playing a joke on me, that surely God wouldn't tell me something involving my mother without letting her in on his plan. I figured he knew that she would need lots of convincing!

"I have no idea what you're talking about, Matthew," she said, handing me a bag full of groceries to carry inside.

"But God said that you were going to be buy me a stuffed groundhog."

"No, Matthew, *you* said that it would happen; God doesn't lie. When he makes a promise, he doesn't break it!" As we walked from the car into the house, I got lectured on my selfish need of constantly *wanting* something and also about how her trips to the store weren't always about what *I* wanted. And of course, I already knew that, but Mom was always really good at beating a dead horse. It just didn't make sense to me that God would tell me something and it wouldn't happen; I really believed that God had spoken to me.

"You should be a veterinarian!" I heard the big booming voice say to me once when I was twelve years old. Over the years, God's voice became much friendlier than in years past. "You really ought to consider that, Matthew; you totally *love* animals! I think it seems like a perfect fit to me. You should do it!"

"But I hate the sight of blood," I said, having developed with age the ability to talk back at the voice once in a while. But it was a consistent voice, at times, almost nagging.

"Yeah, but you love cute little puppies and kittens," it said back to me. "And veterinarians get paid very well. You'd be able to support your family! It would make your dad very proud."

The big voice was always very kind, and sometimes it "spoke" inside my head with a British dialect; and for some reason, when it did, the dialect made it sound more intelligent, kind of like Sean Connery in *First Knight*.

But I swear, the voice I heard was also quite fickle; it changed its mind more than a politician. After it got tired of telling me to be a veterinarian, it told me to be a singer. After it told me to be a singer, it told me to pursue banking. And after that, for about three weeks, I heard it say: "Be a pharmacist, Matthew!"

I kind of liked that idea. For some reason, I thought it would be cool to always have to wear a white coat.

However, that idea didn't last very long, mostly because I ended up hearing my calculus professor tell me, "There's no way you're going to pass my class," which made becoming a pharmacist pretty much out of the question. At the time, my teacher's words were just as convincing as what I was hearing from the voice formerly known as God. Eventually, I did learn that the voice I heard wasn't God's voice. That tidbit of wisdom came to me with age. But I think distinguishing between God and your own inside voice is a difficult task.

But despite it being a little difficult from time to time, I do believe that God leads us and that he communicates with humanity through various means. While I don't know if God carries on continuous conversations with people, like Jansen's conversation with the "voice," I can tell you that I have experienced definitive moments in my life where I have felt God's leading. Most of the time these kinds of events happen during a time of prayer and/or meditation.

Meet Michelle Bennett. You probably know somebody just a little like Michelle. And if you don't, you should. She's fantastic. Michelle is the kind of girl whose hair is a constant testing ground for the latest haircut, dye, or fad. Sure, she's had a mishap or two, like the time she dyed her hair electric blonde and cut it so short that she looked like a Tinkerbellish David Bowie. But normally, Michelle's hair makes a lot of girls a little envious—if not for the style, for her guts.

Michelle and I became friends when we worked together at a Christian ministry in Northern Virginia. We didn't work together for long though, because Michelle switched jobs almost as often as she switched hair color, always looking for what God had planned for her life. (That's my assessment, not necessarily hers.) I reconnected with the now thirtysomething a few months back, and we talked about how her perspective regarding hearing God had changed since her college days.

As we sat in a poorly lit coffeehouse, staring at each other's blank faces, I decided to get "deep" for a moment. "Michelle, can I ask a question: Do you still hear from God?"

"Yes, of course," she said back to me without hesitation, really wanting me to be convinced.

"Hmm. Okay, but do you think your perspective on hearing God has changed since you were in college?" I asked.

"Well, yeah, I think so," she said, this time a little more hesitantly than before. "I think when I was in college I had this notion that God would one day show me exactly what I was supposed to be doing— that if I somehow just trusted and followed him, I would eventually end up in whatever job/career/place I was supposed to end up and that I would be happy. That's what I had always been taught to believe."

"And now, how do you view it?" I asked.

She laughed, giving me a look that said, *Why are you asking me this stuff?*

I didn't tell her that I was writing a book—that is, until after I finished my interview.

"You know, I think I've finally come to understand that I can't simply trust and follow. I mean, yes, those are great things, and they will always be some of the basics for a close walk with God, but I've learned that I actually have to *do* something. You know? It's easy to say, 'Oh, I trust and follow.' But I had to start asking, 'Do I do something when I trust and follow?' I guess I believe that Jesus called me to serve, so I have to serve."

"Do you hear God now?"

"Uh, well, I don't think that hearing from God is some abstract *I'll figure it out one day when I get a sign* type of hearing. Does that make sense? To me, it's more like listening for the gentle everyday whisper of his calling me into service, whether that's in my home life, work life, social life, or humanitarian life. I believe he's constantly asking me to put my own agendas aside and just do what I know he wants me to do. That sounds too easy, doesn't it?"

"Not at all. What you're saying is great! By the way, this is going in a book."

"Oh, nice! I've never been in a book."

(She's lying; I've totally written about her before. She just doesn't know it.)

I will be the first to admit that I'm just a little too spiritually needy at times. But you know, I don't think it's a crime to once in a while crave some kind of burning-bush-type proof that God is with me or that it's his voice I'm hearing. Don't we all need that once in a while? Maybe a talking donkey or the water in my tub to split into two. I just want to know that it's his "gentle whisper" that I'm hearing and not my own (or some other idiot's). And once in a while I get a small sign that I'm hearing God—that I can trust the "voice."

About two weeks prior to losing my job at *CCM*, I found a five-dollar bill lying on the ground in a parking garage. "Yes!" I thought. I don't know what is it about finding abandoned cash that makes the heart leap for joy. But it does seem to work that way, even when it's only a Lincoln that I find. I picked up the crinkled bill and put it in my pocket. As I walked to my car, something inside my gut said to me, "That money is not for you." I'm not sure I can even call what I heard a voice; it was more like a passing thought, one that I couldn't get out of my head.

I was meeting a friend for dinner that evening, so I got into my car and drove to a nearby steak house. Since I was early, I sat in my car and listened to the radio for a moment. By the time I got out of my car to walk into the restaurant, I had forgotten about the five dollars. When I had almost reached the front door, a kid riding a bike stopped me.

"Sir," he said, "my school is raising money for underprivileged kids …"

I didn't even let him finish his pitch; I reached into my back pocket, pulled out the bill, and handed it to him.

"Kid, I've got your money right here," I said.

"Oh, wow, thank you, sir!"

And I know this might sound cheesy, but then I looked at the kid and said, "No, thank you."

And then he rode off, perhaps on his way to Burger King to buy a hamburger and fries or perhaps, something far worse like crack cocaine—quite honestly, I didn't care. I looked up at the sky (as you know, that's where God lives) and said out loud, "Thank you, God; you have no idea how much I needed to know that it was you I was hearing." But then again, maybe he did know that I needed a little nudge.

And perhaps he needed to see that I was still willing to hear him.

My Questions for You

1. Do you spend time on a regular basis meditating and/or praying?

2. Is any of that time spent listening?

3. What kind of "signs" (if any) has God given you to let you know that you are hearing him?

The Word of God Speaks

As far as I'm concerned, my friend Chris Seay isn't your average American pastor. There are many reasons I believe that: 1) He's far too comfortable in his own skin. 2) He knows far too much about foreign beer. 3) His church—a group of people called Ecclesia in Houston— looks like a rundown warehouse from the outside, a building that, even if you're looking for it, you might miss. Over the past couple of years, because he invited me to participate in a translation of the Bible he's dubbed *The Voice*, I've gotten to know Chris quite well. We talked last year in California at a conference for pastors.

"Chris, can I just say this? You don't act very Christian in my opinion," I said.

He laughed.

"Well, depending on what you mean by that," he replied, "I might take it as a compliment!"

"Good. It is a compliment."

Every time I'm in the same room as this man, I ask God to please let some of what he has rub off on me. I'm serious. There's an uncanny contentment, peace, and strength that Chris seems to have that I want. He seems more like a Buddhist than a Christian to me. I'm not sure that will make sense to you, but really, it explains him perfectly. Maybe I need to find new Christian friends, but most of the Buddhists I know are much more Jesus-like than a lot of the Christians who hang around me.

Chris is passionate about the power of Scripture. When I visited Ecclesia, I heard him tell his congregation that when we come in contact with the story of God, we should be changed. "Sometimes when you're reading Scripture," he said, "you have to ask God, 'What do you want me to learn from this?' I believe the Spirit of God reveals that to an open heart. I am going to read this passage from Psalms three times. As you close your eyes and listen to these words being spoken, I want you to first ask God to reveal to you one word out of this passage that says something to you."

The word I heard was *sustain*.

"I am going to read this passage again," said Chris, "and this time, I want you to ask God to give you a phrase."

My phrase was "You will sustain me, oh God."

"Now, lastly, as I read this chapter one final time, I want you to ask God how these words should cause you to live differently. Let the Holy Spirit speak to you."

That final reading was moving for me. When I was in Houston, I was going through a time of questioning, maybe an experience that was not unlike the one the psalmist was walking through. As I listened for how God wanted me to allow this passage to change my life, I again heard clearly a voice telling me to remember that in whatever circumstance I am in, my God will be my foundation, that he would be my life support.

I've often thought that life would be simpler if there were a formula that one could follow when listening for God's voice. Maybe a phone number would help or perhaps a MySpace page. But let's face it; if we were given a sure way of hearing from God, more than likely we'd probably still find some way to complicate it. Or just not listen. Though I've heard an awful lot of people offer equations for how God interacts with us, the blueprints they offer usually come with big promises that don't seem to work for everyone. And to be honest, I'm kind of thankful there isn't a formula.

But the story of God as written down in Scripture is clear about one thing: God interacts with people. People experience him many different ways. And like I said, I've often mistaken my own thoughts or other people's advice for the voice of God. But over time, as I've experienced what I believe to be God speaking into my life, I've learned a few things. God's voice is consistent. In other words, it doesn't tell you something one week and then tell you something new the next. I think sometimes we get so antsy to hear

God speak that we sometimes project our own thoughts and ideas onto him. Because let's face it, telling people "God said it" is a great excuse to utilize from time to time. It's easy to do; plus, it's difficult for somebody to argue with somebody when they're telling you that it's *God's will*. I've also learned that when God wants me to hear him, he makes that message loud and clear. There's no guesswork when God speaks. You know it's him, because God doesn't play games with us.

Of course, we may like to pretend that he handles his relationships like we handle ours—fickle and unsure. Although God knows and understands humanity, he doesn't do things like humanity. He doesn't manipulate; if we don't hear him the first time, more than likely, he'll speak again. When he's letting us in on his will, he isn't concerned with gaining our approval. And he isn't controlled by time. I think we should take comfort in those things. And we should pursue listening for his voice accordingly. We should seek him, serve him, and believe him. The last thing I've learned about hearing God is this: When he does speak, it's usually not about me. I'd often prefer it to be about me, but it's more than often not. It's normally about me getting out of my comfort zone and serving God by serving another person.

But please, don't read me wrong: I don't hear God all the time. In other words, he and I aren't in constant conversation. We have our moments. Some people claim that they are in consistent talks with the Almighty, and I don't want to discount their claims. All I know is that I believe God communicates with people. And for me, I've been able to hear him more clearly when I'm at a place where I was comfortable with how he made me to hear him. I believe he's made all of us to hear him in different ways. And consequently, how *you* hear from God may be different than how somebody else hears and interacts with God. He didn't make us all to interact with him the same way, so I think that we should be free enough to engage God in a way that's comfortable for each of us.

everybody needs a Yoda

What cannot be achieved in one lifetime will happen
when one lifetime is joined to another.

—HAROLD KUSHNER

I'm just going to go ahead and admit this right at the beginning: This chapter has the potential to become just a little bit cheesy. Believe me, if it happens, it won't be on purpose. I hate schmaltzy spiritual-relationship chapters just like the next person. For some reason whenever Christian writers—*sometimes (gasp!), even me*—start editorializing about the importance of relationships and community and small groups and all that friendship blah blah blah, our words usually end up coming across like a literary version of Dionne Warwick's hit song "That's What Friends Are For." No offense to lovable and psychic-friendly Dionne, but no writer wants their book compared to an '80s power ballad vocalized by Whitney Houston's cousin. (Yet, I'd be a total hypocrite if I didn't admit that once in a while I fall prey to Dionne's tune "I Say a Little Prayer.") But despite some relationship banter making me want to watch *Brady Bunch* reruns, *relationships* and, yes, even *community* are two of the most important facets of life. Though somebody in the church needs to find a new word that could describe the ongoing gathering and loving of people, without relational community our stories would be quite boring and uneventful. So, Dionne's sort of right: *That's what friends are for.*

One thing I have learned in my own personal stroll through life is this: A crucial part of our calling is very much dependent on how we interact with the people that God puts on the path with us, beside us, and even behind us. Sometimes these people come into our lives only for a season. And sometimes, these people walk the curious path with us for a lifetime. Whatever the case might be, an important part of your calling is building, serving, encouraging, and empowering your relationships with others.

The Bible talks a lot about the good and the bad of relationships; in fact, a "relationship thread" is written into almost every story within Scripture. Think about it: From the first male/female relationship that we read about in Genesis 1 to the friendship/bond that existed between King David and Jonathan to the mentor/student relationship of the prophets Elijah and Elisha, God's story is often told through the trials, temptations, adventures, and/or the fulfillment that people discovered in relationships. Even Jesus' ministry and message while he lived on earth was grounded in the importance of relationship. Consider how he lived his life. This is something that you have more than likely heard before, but it's worth repeating: Jesus valued people above everything except the relationship with his Father. Some of the relationships Jesus valued were individuals he pulled out of the crowd and called to be disciples; others he called to contribute to the kingdom that he was building on earth. Each of Jesus' relationships were important—perhaps not equally so—but important nonetheless. Since it's our goal to live out the teachings of Jesus in our daily lives, I tend to think that if we're not playing a hopeful role in building community, then we're missing one of Jesus' most valued messages.

In thinking about our calling, the human relationships that develop throughout our lives will play different roles. Sometimes the people we know will be cheerleaders or confidants. Sometimes they will be spiritual or professional mentors (sometimes both). Sometimes they will be our leaders or our followers or people we are called to serve. No matter what role they play in our lives, how we view, perceive, pursue, serve, and cherish our relationships affects the outcome of our stories. It affects our calling. It reveals the truth about whether or not we're truly curious.

My Questions for You

1. What are your main objectives when it comes to building relationships? In other words, do you have any relational "goals"?

2. What qualities do you see in the way Jesus developed relationships that you would most like to emulate?

3. Think about your current relationships for a moment. How many of them push you to be all that you are "called" to be?

The Secrets of the Jedi

No matter where you are in your life, you need help. No, really, you do. That might sound a little hopeless to you, but nonetheless, it's true:

You need some guidance. Not once in a while. Not sometimes. All the time. This is true for each and every one of us: You need a mentor. Maybe a couple of them.

I believe I was eight years old when I saw the Star Wars movie *The Empire Strikes Back* for the first time. Like most kids during that time, I was fascinated by all things Star Wars. While I wasn't allowed to watch the movie in the theaters (*long* story), I watched that movie over and over on VHS. Anyway, when I first watched the part of the movie where Luke Skywalker and R2-D2 venture alone to the marshy planet of Dagobah so that Luke can undergo some advanced Jedi training, Yoda's (Luke's mentor and Jedi master, for those of you who have never seen the movie, which might be a sin) somewhat cryptic way of advising young Skywalker frustrated me much like it frustrated Luke. But, as those who have seen the movie know, Luke didn't go to Dagobah with humility. Because of his pride and cockiness and lack of patience, Yoda didn't believe he was ready to learn the secrets of the Jedi. Eventually, in *The Return of the Jedi*, Luke goes back to Yoda, but on that first visit, Luke wasn't ready for a mentor. He wasn't ready to learn.

When I was twenty years old, somebody very wise gave me some good advice: "Matthew," this person said to me, "always have somebody who is older and wiser speaking into your life—somebody who will give you good advice and point out your flaws when you're wrong and direct you back to truth. *That's* how to live successfully; learn from somebody else's story." That's been some of the most valuable advice I've ever received. I hope somebody has given you that advice along the way, and you've made a point to apply it to your own personal story. But no matter what spot you are at in life, I don't think it's ever too late to begin. In my own life, I've always attempted to heed this advice. The mentors I have known have made a huge difference in my life, adding to very important chapters within my story.

My first mentor was a woman I interned for at the Gospel Music Association when I was a second-semester junior in college. Kristy Nelson hired me after I answered her ad at Belmont's internship office. When I interviewed with her, her business demeanor as well as her knowledge of the music industry instantly intrigued me. During the two semesters that I worked under her leadership, our relationship was more like a friendship than a boss/employee relationship. At the time I didn't know much about *how* to pursue a mentor, and so, before I left my position, I just talked to her about whether or not she would be willing to meet with me on occasion, allow me to talk to her about my career choices, and bounce ideas off of her from time to time. She agreed. For a couple of years, I met with her sporadically and sought her advice about my life as it related to school and career. Many times, she just shared wisdom by telling me about her personal experiences. Our meetings weren't businesslike or overtly serious; we were just two friends—one of which was older and more experienced in the professional world—talking about our lives. Probably one of the most important aspects of my relationship with Kristy was the validation that I received from her. Though at the time I didn't realize the importance of being professionally validated by someone in the industry I was interested in, when I look back I realize that often I found the courage to take career risks because of the conversations I had with Kristy. Her support and advice affected the initial steps of my career path more than I would have ever realized at the time.

A good friend of mine is a film student who lives in the Los Angeles area. Once, when he and I were chatting about the frustrations regarding his career choice, I asked him if he had a mentor. "I'm working on it," said Daniel. "Out here you have to be very careful how you pursue those kinds of relationships. People are leery of those who want to *learn*! They're fearful that you're just trying to get something out of them. But I eventually found somebody who was willing to give me a chance and trust me." He laughed.

"How did it end up happening?" I asked.

"Well, I started researching the names of people in this town whom I would want to emulate," he said. "You know, keeping my eyes open for people with talent who also have a little integrity. And in Hollywood, the talent is easy to find, but the integrity part tends to be difficult. When I met a couple of people who I wanted to get to know a little more, I sent them both e-mails, explained who I was, what I was hoping to do some day, and asked them if there would be any way I could buy them lunch at some point."

"Did you get any response?"

"From one of them, I did," he said. "But that was okay. Because the guy who did e-mail me back was the one I liked the best anyway. He and I ended up having lunch on a Saturday. That first time, I just asked him questions about his work, how he got into the industry— made it all about him! People in this town *love* to talk about themselves. Actually, I kind of think that's true anywhere. So, that's what I did; I let him talk about himself for a couple of hours and just listened. We're pretty good friends now, and he's an awesome mentor. He's taught me a lot—given me some very cool opportunities. And I've been very protective of his time, and because of *who* he is, I'm also protective of his name. *I'm not a name dropper.*" (And he's not; I still don't know the name of his mentor.)

But Daniel raises an important concern for many. Each industry has specific good and bad ways to connect with a professional mentor. So, it's important you learn the art of connecting with someone in whatever field you might be going into. And once you have a mentor, make sure you protect the relationship, don't overuse it; and respect the professional boundaries of the relationship.

A Spiritual Mentor

But having a mentor isn't just about your professional life; it's also important to your journey and to your story to have a spiritual mentor. When I was working at Jammin' Java in Chester, Maryland, we had a pretty extensive guitar shop that was adjacent to the coffeehouse. All Geared Up was the brainchild of Brian Bowdren, a prominent forty-something businessman who was also an avid guitar and bass player. His dream was to one day retire early and spend his days building high-end bass guitars. Brian went to my church. Over time, he and I became close friends. On many occasions, Brian and I would sit around and talk about life with each other. We'd talk about work. We'd talk about relationships—working relationships, women, church politics, and otherwise. But most importantly, Brian and I talked about God. We spent a lot of time asking each other hard questions about the spiritual journey. Oftentimes, I was able to talk to Brian about the more personal stuff that was going on in my spiritual life—the *why* questions, *how* questions, and a lot of the questions that I wasn't able to talk about with anybody else. *Why was I able to do this?* Because over time, Brian and I built a trust with each other, and also, because I admired the man that he was. (Brian passed away suddenly in 2004.) I wanted him speaking into my life.

Curious People: Daphne

Daphne is a mom of two boys and spends most of her daytimes being a mother, which she believes is her most important role other than being a wife to her husband, Jonathan. She and I met years ago—we're not best friends—but close enough that when we see each other, there's always something to talk about. One of life's areas that she's very passionate about is the volunteer job that she does for her church—a mentoring program that aims at pairing young men and young women with "more mature" men and women for spiritual mentoring. I asked Daphne a few questions for this book.

> **MATTHEW:** What do you look for in somebody who wants to be a spiritual mentor?

> **DAPHNE:** Well, it's not like we're looking for perfection or whatever. But we are looking for men and women who are journeying with God on a deep and sincere level. I think something else we're looking for is a certain amount of maturity, because they have to be able to understand that some of the young adults might be in a different

place spiritually or going through major questions or other life issues. So, we want them to be able to handle those kinds of situations, and *not* feel like they are there to fix everything.

MATTHEW: How do you make the process not feel a little calculated? "Pairing people up" seems a little formulaic to me.

DAPHNE: Oh, we think that too. The only people who sign up are those who want to be trained as mentors; we do not actually introduce the two individuals to each other. We let that happen naturally. But the program is talked about a lot, so we have a good number of people participating.

MATTHEW: What advice do you have for people in their twenties and early thirties who are looking for a mentor? In other words, what qualities make a good mentoree?

DAPHNE: I think patience and grace are always good qualities to have. Remember, the people who are mentoring you aren't perfect people. Also, you have to be teachable and humble about where you are in your story. Nobody has all the answers, but some people kind of like to think they do.

Like I wrote earlier, Scripture mentions all kinds of relationships, but I think the mentor-student relationship is outlined more often than many of the other types. Consider Moses' mentoring of Joshua. The two followers of God had a unique relationship in that they served each other, one by mentoring, the other by being an honorable and respectful mentoree. What I love about that story is Joshua's proactive desire to be around Moses, to help him, to serve him. It wasn't simply a *get all you can before he dies* type of relationship. I believed he *loved* Moses, and it was out of love that he desired to glean all that he could from the man of God. Joshua grew mentally, physically, and spiritually because of his respect for Moses.

I think that's an important idea for you to grasp: having a mentor isn't simply about *receiving* wisdom; it's also about you playing an active role in serving that individual. A few months ago, I met a forty-something Hindu man (Dakshi) in the gym sauna. I'd seen the man before, but I'd never had an opportunity to chat with him at length. When I did, Dak (the name he asked me to call him) and an older Caucasian gentleman were talking about their upcoming journey to India, Dak's home country. As I sat and eavesdropped on their conversation, the two laughed and talked like they'd known each other for years. When he returned, I was able to talk with him.

"How was your trip back to India?" I asked Dak.

"Oh, we had a splendid time!" he said. "How did you know I just returned?"

"I saw you at the gym with the older gentleman who went with you."

"Oh, yes," said Dak. "*Yeah*, William went with me. It was his first time in India. And he just *loved* it."

"How do the two of you know each other?" I asked.

"We've been friends for years," said Dak thoughtfully. "Nearly thirty years."

"That's amazing."

"Yeah, when I moved to Chattanooga for my first year of residency, William was one of the senior doctors at the hospital. Because I was hurting for money, he and his wife let me live with them. They became my dear friends—like family really. He is a real mentor in my life."

"Wow," I said. "What's the age difference, if you don't mind me asking?"

"Twenty-seven years!" he said, "Yeah, William and I are like father and son. In fact, just last week, William was put in the hospital with heart issues and his son called me because he said I would be the only one who could talk him into receiving the treatment the doctors were recommending. So, I went down to Chattanooga and spent some time with him."

"Did he get the procedure?"

"Oh, yes," said Dak. "And it looks like he's going to be just fine! I'd do anything for that man and he for me—he's made a huge difference in my personal story."

Remember, a mentor relationship isn't simply about "getting," and it's not simply about "giving" (and here's where the *cheese* begins), it's about living.

My Questions for You

1. When you think about a mentoring relationship, what first comes to mind?

2. What do you believe is "your role" in this kind of relationship?

3. Do you have a mentor? What have you learned from him or her? How do you serve him or her?

Walking with Others

I believe that doing life *with people* always beats the alternative. Now, please note that I said *I believe*, which doesn't imply that I always do it or that I think it's easy. But from my own personal experiences, I can always say having company along for the journey was better than walking alone. But walking through life with company at your side is often not the easier way to live. But still, I think it's the best way to live.

If you're a human being, and forgive me for assuming that most of you are, you are impacted on various levels by relationships and/or community. *Big surprise*, huh? Okay, not really. But the influence of relationships is probably even deeper and more potent than we could ever imagine. It affects our spiritual health. It affects our mental and emotional stability. It can make us feel physically strong or it can make us feel weak. Relationships have that kind of power.

Because the relationships we pursue (or the ones that seem to be attached to us) impact us so deeply, it's no shock that our relationships would also have a pretty extensive impact on how we perceive and pursue our callings. In other words, when we feel confident and loved by people, we're more apt to be spiritually, mentally, emotionally, and physically capable of venturing on the curious path toward living our calling. That's how God has designed us to be—people who are affected (on a varying number of degrees) by other people. And like I said, the impact can be positive, negative, or um, kind of obsolete. Most of us have experienced (or currently are experiencing) all three of those types of relationships.

HOKEY MOMENT

What "negative" relationships do you have in your life right now? You know, the people who pull you down, drain you, or make you feel less than alive. The truth is, that person could be anyone from a boyfriend to a father to a boss at work. And oftentimes, we don't have the option to just drop that person out of our lives. But we can learn how to manage that relationship. Don't be afraid to seek the help of a pastor or counselor or medical professional in learning how to deal with your frustrating relationships. You can't let one person's actions—no mater who that person is—dictate who you are and what you're able to accomplish.

Curious People: John, a Homeless

When I was in Houston recently, I met John. And despite this vibrant soul not having a regular place to sleep at night or knowing where his next meal would come from, he had a lot to say about what he believes is the community of faith's responsibility to those who are less fortunate.

MATTHEW: John, can you tell me what the most difficult part about being homeless is?

JOHN: Oh, there are many parts of it that are hard. I mean, it's hard to smell so bad that people don't want to sit too close to you. (Laughs) I hate when I have to walk three or four miles just to get a shower. But I do it. Because sometimes you just have to. But the most difficult part for me is seeing the way people look at me and prejudge me without really knowing who I am. Most people don't care enough about me to even stop me and ask me my name. That's hard. I guess because they think I'm out on the streets begging for food that I'm automatically categorized into a certain group of people who have nothing to offer society. But that's just not right, you know, man? They have no idea that I fought in Vietnam. I gave nearly five years of my life to that good-for-nothing war. But that's a different story, Matthew. You just watch people, you'll see them stare at me; I've gotten so I can see what they think about me written in their eyes.

MATTHEW: Do you ever see "Jesus" out on these streets?

JOHN: I'm assuming you mean through people, right?

MATTHEW: Yeah, that's what I mean.

JOHN: I do see "Jesus" walking around on these streets. There are a lot of very nice people in Houston—*godly people*—people who care about others who are less fortunate. But to be honest, I don't see him enough. You know, I believe in what the Holy Scriptures say. I believe with all of my heart that the poor were very special to Jesus, that he wants us to take care of each other. Isn't that what being Christian is all about? That's why I'm always telling other homeless guys that they're special to Jesus. But sadly, they don't believe me half the time.

MATTHEW: Really? Why is that?

JOHN: Because they see how a lot of Christians treat them. Sometimes it's just awful, Matthew. There are a lot of churches in this city. There are so many churches that I'm not sure there should ever be somebody who goes to bed hungry or is left out in the cold. And when I read the words of Jesus, I'm convinced that you can't truly call yourself a Christian and ignore the needs that are right there in front of your face. Can you? If you ask me, Jesus was so clear about taking care of the poor.

MATTHEW: Do you think taking care of the poor should be considered a part of our natural calling as followers of Jesus?

JOHN: Absolutely. Whenever Jesus interacted with people, he took care of them. That was one of the first things Jesus did. Before preaching at 'em, he'd feed them or take care of their most obvious needs. You see, a lot of Christians today think that Christianity is there to fill their needs, when Christians are actually here to fill other people's needs.

MATTHEW: John, what's your vision for the future? Where do you want to be in five years?

JOHN: I want to get off the streets! I want to not be addicted to alcohol. But I know that I'll need somebody's help before I can do that. But you know, until that happens, I also want to be a reflection of Jesus while I'm out here. I think I'm here for a reason. That's for sure. And two, I want to become a construction worker.

MATTHEW: That's awesome, man. What kind of construction work do you want to do?

JOHN: I want to build homes. I hope someday I can build my own.

Why You Gotta Go and Make Things So Complicated?

The impact of human relationship on our stories is a very complicated topic. Just ask Avril Lavigne. There are many reasons this could be the case. For starters, each of us develops relationships according to our own personal experiences; in other words, it's a learned trait that we pick up from our environment, parents, church, or friends. Plus, all of us have tendencies to make different kinds of choices when it comes to relationships. In fact, even our motives for making our relationship choices vary widely. So, when you combine all of those realities with the fact that some of the relationships we are managing are not of our choosing—in other words, family, fellow employees, your best friend's girlfriend (or boyfriend)—it's not too difficult to see how it all can get rather complicated at times.

Sometimes the complications can become so overwhelming that you find yourself flirting with the idea of becoming one of those freaks who lives a secluded life somewhere in the backwoods of Montana (think *Unabomber!*). You know, the kind of person who only comes out of hiding when he or she learns that a family member is dying or gets profiled on *Dateline's* "To Catch a Predator" series. Yes, a life of seclusion can become *that* frightening, and not to mention, it can look rather icky on a résumé. But sometimes even the most fellowship savvy of us have moments when we are tempted to consider moving away to New Zealand or Galápagos Islands just to get a break from, *um*, "fellowship."

Do you get this way sometimes? Sure, some of you probably move away to some place like Sri Lanka or Nebraska rather than New Zealand, but do you get the sentiment? However, the large majority of us never run. We never go into hiding. *Why?* For one, it isn't practical for the majority of us. (Have you seen the dollar's foreign exchange rate lately?) And two, most of us don't have that option, and even if we did have the means to move somewhere secluded, we wouldn't truly be secluded because we'd struggle giving up our addiction to Facebook. I mean, even with dial-up, you can poke a friend or two from 8,000 miles away, and if you're game, throw a sheep at them just for kicks.

But why do we want to run sometimes? Well, again, community is complicated. In most of the world's developed cultures, where our idea of community tends to be a cul-de-sac and Fourth of July picnics, true community isn't something that comes easy for the majority of us. We're too independent, too individualistic, too self-assured, too capitalistic to *truly* know what the human need for community is all about. In fact, some of us have moments when we are down right terrible at it. But we can't simply blame it on the culture that we have grown up in. Our breakdown in experiencing community is also because we're human beings, which means we're sometimes prone to relational mistakes, depression, narcissism, and/or unhealthy emotional neediness, and the people we hang with are working through similar if not exactly the same issues. No wonder we sometimes find ourselves disillusioned with our community. Many of us go through seasons when we feel like we don't belong, like we're simply existing, fumbling through the motions of community, and reaping very few of its "promised" rewards. But instead of running away from our "community"—most of us end up doing one of three things: 1) We do our best to function, pretending that life is grand within the confines of what we've been told is God's ideal "Christian community." 2) We invent our own form of seclusion in the comfort of our own homes (or for some, in the comfort of being anonymous in chat rooms and online forums). 3) We see this life with God as a journey, one where we are constantly living and learning (and sometimes *reliving* and *relearning*) how God has designed true community to be.

So you might be thinking that, now that I've outlined a few

reasons why community is a rather complex topic for so many of us to think about and even *more difficult* for us to live, I'm now going to tell you five easy ways you can pursue a good type of community, the kind that will make the curious path a beautiful journey and your calling everything it's meant to be. And if I knew the "secret" to the perfect community, I would certainly tell you all about it. But honestly, I don't know what the ideal Christian community looks like in the twenty-first century. While some people today believe true community is about a family living intentionally in one big house with lots of other people around all the time, others think it's a two-hour Bible study on Tuesday evenings at 7:30. And I know some who think it's a family reunion that happens on the third weekend each June, and still, I have a friend who says I will never know what true biblical community looks like until I visit his town in Sweden. Truthfully, God's idea of community is probably all of the above as much as it is *none of the above.*

Community is different for all of us, I believe. Like most of the complicated parts of life, community is a spiritual journey that shouldn't be watered down into four simple rules. From my experience, that journey depends on two things: 1) a person's own experiences and environment, and 2) the condition of a person's heart. Where we live, the church we go to, and the season we are living in will all affect how we are able to experience and pursue community. For the Pentecostal living in San Diego, community will look very differently from for the Emergent guy who goes to college in New Hampshire. And I think that's okay. Sure, some of what you pursue— the ideals of Jesus that people attempt to emulate—will be similar, but how you live those ideals out might be very different. As odd as it might seem, how people venture into their understanding of godly community is a personal journey, one that begins in a person's heart. When Jesus taught the Sermon on the Mount, the majority of his message was about a human's heart condition; the same is true in regards to our view of community. Since community is about serving people, a person with a selfish or angry or bitter outlook isn't going to have a healthy mind-set about their calling to be communal. But I believe if a person truly pursues journeying with God, the missional experience of interacting with people through true community will become an avid part of their calling.

A Personal Lesson in Community

When I lived in Washington, D.C., during my midtwenties, I began to learn (and relearn) what community is all about or at least something about it. Early on during my job at Vienna, Virginia's Jammin' Java, my boss introduced me to my friend Daniel; he was an intern for a summer at the coffeehouse. The two of us became close almost immediately. Over good food and better drink, Daniel and I had conversations about faith, life, doubt, and temptations. We told each other our past stories—the good ones and also the not-so-good ones. We introduced each other to our friends. Sooner or later, there were ten or twelve of us who were very close, a group of people who did life together. We went to dance clubs with each other. We ran church youth programs together. We conversed at bars together. We encouraged each other. We cheered for each other. We prayed for each other. We worshipped Jesus together. It did not matter that many of us worshipped at different churches on Sunday mornings just like it did not matter that we worked different jobs Monday through Friday. Those types of differences didn't limit our ability to commune with each other. I'd be lying if I didn't admit that it took some time for me to learn my complete role in the lives of these people. In fact, sometimes I'm still learning my role in the lives of my closest community. They become a part of who I am and what I'm doing. Even though many of my friends are scattered across the country, we still need each other and our bond remains strong. And I honestly think that's just a small taste of community, just the beginning.

Community requires selflessness. It requires being able to serve others unconditionally. I've learned that when I allow myself to be embraced by that kind of community and at the same time I am attempting to embrace that kind of community, I get a glimpse of what life is all about.

My Questions for You

1. How do you define *community?*

2. What have been your main frustrations regarding your community?

3. How fulfilling is the community that you're experiencing right now?

waiting on God is a contact sport

I grew up with six brothers.
That's how I learned to dance—waiting for the bathroom.

—BOB HOPE

When I was twenty-three and just out of college, I was cocky enough to believe my life was about to become a whole lot easier. No more professors. No more tests. No more college drama. Though I hadn't figured out where I'd be working after graduation, I expected to land my dream job—or at least, something that would lead me toward my dream job—by the end of that first summer out of Belmont.

Upon graduating, I started using my hard-earned degree in business (with a concentration in the music industry) by getting a job as a server at a moderately high-end restaurant in Nashville called Café Milano. While my degree didn't really come in handy when describing how delightful the mussels appetizer tasted (the little guys were steamed with garlic) or when I was rolling my fifty place settings of silverware at the end of my shift, it gave me a little clout when some of Nashville's most powerful music business gurus sat down at my tables. Secretly, as I worked at keeping them drunk and fat, I hoped that when they heard my story about wanting to work in the music business, they would offer me a position at the record label or publishing company where they worked—or at least some encouragement or advice that would give me a little hope.

All of those businessmen and women must have forgotten that at one time in their lives they too were getting nowhere fast, because just like those who came into the restaurant from insurance companies or banks, the music business peeps just ended up asking for more water or lemons.

To me, the life of a server was too much like that of a vampire—sleeping during the daytime and working until ungodly hours at night—but I still enjoyed it. I liked making people happy. And the money wasn't bad. However, despite liking my job and actually being pretty good at it, my surroundings still felt very dark. After about a month or two, I stopped trying to impress the music business folks; a part of me just decided to own my place in this world. "I'm a server," I said to myself. "I make decent money. And I work around some very fascinating people who seem to understand me." And too, there was a girl whose southern personality wooed my heart. But the more I tried to talk myself into sitting back and enjoying the life that I was living, the more I felt like I was taking a wrong turn in slow motion.

That "voice" inside kept telling me that if I didn't want to wake up at the age of thirty as a server, I needed to do something drastic. But I tried to shut it up, because the words it spoke were hardly comforting.

Do something drastic.

Over and over again I would feel that same message sitting in my gut like yesterday's Papa John's. Instead of helping me feel clarity, that voice made me feel messed up. In fact, there were times when I would walk into my apartment at three o'clock in the morning after having worked a twelve-hour shift and I'd fall down on my bed and cry because of how lost I felt. I was twenty-three and very confused. I was fearful that "drastic" meant that I would have to leave Nashville, my college friends, and my codependence to a dead-end job, and I didn't know where I'd go. During that time, one of my friends told me that "the world was at my fingertips, that all I had to do was reach for my dreams," but something inside told me that my dreams of working in the music industry were not going to become a reality the way I had planned. Five months after graduating from college, I moved home.

For fourteen months, I worked job after job, hoping that one of them would "feel" like a career. But none of them did. I eventually took a job at a local warehouse where I stood next to people without teeth and without educations and stuffed envelopes. During that time I turned down several job offers. Even though I was making only seven dollars an hour stuffing envelopes, I refused to take another job that I didn't feel called to. So I stayed there and waited for God to show me a sign. And one day I learned that "lost" has its advantages. (To be continued.)

Biding Time

I've spent a good deal of time thinking about how much time the men and women of the Bible spent waiting on God. I mean, consider poor Sarah; she waited a long time before God allowed her to conceive Isaac. This must have been a grueling time for Abraham and Sarah, considering the fact that God had called them to give birth to a mighty nation. That's kind of difficult to do when your womb is barren. But then God entered the picture and said, "You're going to have a bouncing baby boy!" I mean, is it really any wonder the mother of all Jews laughed when she heard Abraham tell her that she was going to give birth to a son? She was ninety! And the effects of menopause had long taken over her body. But no doubt you know how the story ended.

When I read that story, and frankly, many of the stories within Scripture, I have questions: *Why did God make Abraham and Sarah wait? Did the couple have to wait so long? Was God just proving himself with this particular story? If he planned to give them a child, why make them wait?*

Scripture is full of stories that reflect a God who is constantly making people wait. But it's difficult to remain curious when you're waiting on God to move or do some kind of magic trick on your behalf. I know this from experience.

Fourteen months feels just a little bit shorter than eternity when you're trying to figure out what your life is supposed to be about. That could be for a couple of reasons: It might be that fourteen months is actually a long time, or it might just be that the culture we live in makes it feel like it's a long time because we're so used to moving in fast-forward motion. Our lives move at a quicker pace than speeding bullets, a T-3 line, or "Jesus" when he's just finished moving in the 9:30 service and is prepping to do it again at 11:00. And while our parents remember a time when they had moments available to sit around and think, we have to schedule *thinking* time into our calendars. And even then, we can't seem to think without Macs sitting in our laps. Many of us believe that if we don't keep up with the speed of life we'll miss something, or perhaps scarier, we won't be missed.

Waiting can do some crazy things to your brain, especially when it's God you're waiting on. And sometimes other Christians don't help the matter too much. At least forty-two times during the fourteen months that I lived at home with my mother and father not knowing what I was supposed to do or where I was supposed to be, somebody came up to me and said, "Keep waiting on God, Matthew! He'll let you know what to do!" And most of the time, though I wanted to believe that to be true, I thought to myself, *Yeah, right.*

Let me be bluntly honest here: Clichés are nice reminders when you can afford to eat, but they are crappy sentiments when you have no idea what you are doing with your life. Maybe it's just me, but these types of sentiments seem to be pretty trite when you've been hoping for quite some time that God will sooner or later zap something fabulous into your life.

At the time, I didn't know what kind of fabulousness I wanted God to bring into my life, but I certainly had my list of criteria. Just in case he needed my help, I gave God ideas to think about and consider. I'd drop hints about things that I'd be willing to do if he wanted me to. I was willing to go to seminary. I didn't mind going back to college and getting my teaching certification. If he wanted me to, I would have considered a job in sales, especially if he was willing to take into consideration my personal stipulations—the ones I wrote down in a smaller, less obvious print. But from my vantage point, I gave God lots of options.

So there, in the house that I grew up in, sleeping in the same bed that I had slept in when I was five, I waited for God to part a Red Sea in front of me or send fire down from heaven. Sometimes friends would come over to my parents' house and wait with me. To help pass the time, we'd watch movies or play cards or sit around and talk to each other about how *waiting on God* is sometimes not so bad. But eventually, my father got tired of coming home during his lunch break and seeing me wait in front of the television, and that was despite the fact that he too was a fan of *The Price Is Right*.

My Questions for You

1. Think about the last time you went through an experience of *waiting*, what did you end up learning to be true about yourself? What did you learn to be true about God?

2. When you think about the story of Abraham and Sarah *waiting* for a child, what do *you* think God was trying to teach them?

3. Does the thought of waiting scare you? If so, how?

Working Through the Wait

When you're in the process of waiting, it's easy to stop living to some degree. Of course, our hearts continue beating, but instead of living every day with passion, we often just look to the future and think it's not worth being excited about life unless life is perceived to be exciting. I guess that seems logical to some degree. Many of us are the kind of people whose emotional stability tends to hang on whether or not our circumstances are pleasant. But just when I thought my circumstances couldn't get any more professionally grim, something happened. This "something" happened just about two weeks before I was about to enroll at a college where I planned to get my teaching certification. But instead of jumping up and down in a holy fit, I did something that was more like an exasperated grunt. *Finally*, I thought.

I was working my last day at the warehouse (you know, the one with the people who didn't have all their teeth). Well, honestly, I was starting to become kind of comfortable at that place; it had become kind of like a second home. I mean, I knew I didn't want to stuff envelopes for the rest of my life, but I did enjoy getting to know the people. The people who worked at USA Fulfillment were salt-of-the-earth kind of folk, the kind of people who loved you unconditionally as long as you were truthful with them. I learned more than I would have ever believed to be possible from many of those people. One of them was a fortysomething woman name Maryanne. During the ten months that I worked there, she and I had become work buddies. We took breaks together and often shared stories with each other during those breaks.

"Matthew, I'm so sad that you are leaving," she said to me on the day prior to my last. "But I know this isn't where God wants you to be. He's got bigger plans for you."

"I'm gonna miss you, too, Maryanne," I said, unsure whether or not I believed the whole *bigger plans* talk. "I know this place isn't where I'm supposed to be at this time, but I gotta tell you, I really have grown while I was here."

She smiled.

"I wanted to let you know that I was talking about you last night," said Maryanne with a gleam in her eye. "I was on the phone with my friend Terry, telling her all about you. Do you know Terry? She goes to Wye Bible Church."

"I don't *know* her, but I've seen her before," I said, and then I laughed. "So, what were you saying about me?"

"Well, I got to thinking about you and your education and your *huge* potential, and I started wondering if Terry and her husband Paul had any jobs at their company—you know they are the CEOs of one of the largest elder-care facilities in the world—and so, I called her and asked if Paul would talk with you for a few minutes. She told me to give you their number."

"Maryanne, you didn't have to do that!" I said. "But gosh, that is so nice of you."

"Well, I don't know if anything will come out of this, but I figure it couldn't hurt, you know?"

"Well, thank you; this is greatly appreciated."

I didn't know it at the time, but that simple conversation that Maryanne had with Terry Klaassan changed the course of my life. While I didn't end up working for Paul and Terry's Sunrise Assisted Living, ten days later I did have a job as the manager of Jammin' Java, a start-up ministry/coffeehouse that their company funded. That was a job that I ended up doing for almost four years. But like I said, the job changed my life. It put me on a path that I became passionate about, one that combined coffee, music, business, community, ministry, and eventually, writing. I know this to be true: My job at Jammin' Java led to my career as a writer. I'm convinced that I wouldn't be writing this book if Maryanne hadn't had that conversation with Terry. She was the salt of the earth, a woman who brought out God's vivid flavorings in the world around her.

Yes, fourteen months felt like an eternity to me. There were moments when I cried. There were times when I became anxious. There were times when I didn't know if I would ever find myself. But I have to confess: I'm glad that I didn't rush and make any crazy decisions about my future; I'm happy that God didn't give up on me. Sure, I was rather impatient at times during that period of my life, but I think I learned that waiting is sometimes a very good thing. And perhaps we should do it a little more often.

Wrestling with God

As I have written before, each of our stories are unique, and how each of us views God's involvement in them is unique too. But more often than not, at some point in our lives, all of us go through an experience that makes us feel nowhere to be found. For some of us, it's not easy talking about these parts of our stories, mostly because we're not comfortable being lost. But my friend Tommy was willing to talk about the emotional stress of his "lost" experience. Consider the following story:

Other than my wife, Tommy Hall is my closest friend. He's the kind of friend that sticks closer than a brother. The truth is, I'm pretty convinced that Tommy will always be a better person than me. And that's saying something, since once in a while I have moments when I think very highly of myself. But I can't do that when I'm around Tommy. His faith is constantly challenging to me, mainly because he's the guy who is constantly thinking about and trying to help the less fortunate, the underdogs, and people who others find difficult to love. He portrays the kind of compassion that makes a lot of people feel uncomfortable; his faith is foolish in some ways. I mean, the boy still picks up hitchhikers whether they look like America's most wanted or not. Tommy's is the kind of faith that leads him to spend hours with a homeless man or stay night after night with a teenager who's bed-ridden in a hospital. But like all of us, he has his weaknesses, temptations, and trials.

I met Tommy during a period of his life when he spent a good deal of time wading rather hopelessly through depression. Many of those who knew him had no idea what was going on inside of his head and heart. You know, sometimes it's difficult being the guy who everybody loves and who everybody believes they have figured out. And that's Tommy. While at times it's a nice problem to have, at other times it's hard to be honest with yourself and those around you about what you're feeling. Tommy's battle with depression wasn't necessarily constant, but rather the kind that was dependent upon the circumstances he was experiencing. And for several years he fought a secret war inside his own mind about what he was called to do and the frustrations about where he felt his current calling had left him spiritually.

Since I knew all too well what that feels like, and also because I was free enough to be Christian and still talk out loud about my own struggles with depression and anxiety, I became a listening ear for him. I can't tell you how many times we spent an hour or more on the phone learning about God and life through listening to each other's stories.

When I was first getting to know Tommy, I must admit something: I thought his life seemed a little simple. Too simple. I mean, seriously, the place he calls home—Beattyville, Kentucky—is a small community (maybe three thousand people) tucked away in a poor but gorgeous area of the Appalachian Mountains. Only a few months prior to us meeting, the twenty-nine-year-old married Angie, the daughter of his former youth pastor. They live intricately quaint lives in a twelve-hundred-square-foot ranch house that sits on top of a knoll overlooking a frog-filled pond. Angie teaches math at the local high school. On Sundays, they attend a small Bible church that has fifty-some members, bright red pews, and an upright piano. Tommy is the youth pastor at his church, mostly because he's the only one patient enough to do it.

When Tommy and I met, he was a full-time missionary. In fact, for seven years, his daily gig consisted of working at a very conservative Christian camp, the same children's camp where his father got his start in ministry almost thirty years before. As a missionary, he traveled during the fall and winter months with a small band of other missionaries, going into public schools where they would put on Christian puppet shows and teach kids about Jesus. But his passion for mission work came during the summer months when he was a camp counselor, ministering to and serving large and small groups of kids— some of them with special needs—and volunteers from all over the country. Though the summer months were long and grueling, they also made him excited about getting up in the morning. However, his seven years of serving at the camp were beginning to wear him down emotionally, mentally, and spiritually, and slowly, over time, depression set in.

"Don't get me wrong, I've seen some amazing things happen there," he said to me once during one of our many conversations. "I love that place, Matthew. I mean, some of the methods they use to 'share the love of Jesus' make me cringe, but dude, that's my home away from home. I can hardly remember my life without that place."

He stopped for a moment to gather his thoughts.

"But I'm not sure I can do it anymore. I'm tired of being there. Yet it's hard to walk away from a group of people who are like my family. You know what I mean? That's the place where I was called to do ministry. But I don't feel like I belong there anymore. I can't keep faking that I enjoy or feel called to go into schools and do puppet shows. My heart is about helping teenagers; it's always been there."

"I don't understand why you don't just leave, man," I said to him. "I mean, I get the part about you feeling connected to that place, but if you're waking up every day hating the thought of going to work, you should leave. You're not doing them or yourself any favors."

"But I feel trapped," he said.

"Why do you feel trapped?" I asked.

"Dude, for one, I'm not sure I could stand leaving. This might sound dysfunctional, but a part of my identity is in that place, man. And two, *they* will make me feel guilty for even thinking about leaving. And I don't feel like putting up with that."

"Who are *they?*" I asked, giving into my habit of sometimes pushing him too far.

"The directors of the mission. *They* will make life miserable for me."

"Aren't these people Christians? I mean, won't they understand that you just need a change of scenery? Everybody needs a change once in a while"

"You don't get it, bro," he said, sounding somewhat defeated. "I live in a very small town, man. People around here know me as 'the missionary.' I am supposed to live and die here. If I were to leave, do you have any idea what would happen?"

"For one, you would no longer feel trapped," I said, with just a slight bit of passive aggressiveness.

"Again, you don't understand, *Matthew*. People would think I was out of God's will if I were to leave. They would spread rumors about me. You don't know how manipulative some of these people there can be. Okay, I gotta stop. I'm making them sound like horrible people. And they're not; they're good people, bro—just misguided at times."

"You're right. I don't understand. But I do know that you can't live your life based on other people's opinions, man. You weren't made to live that way. In fact, that's not actually living. You were made to be free."

"I know."

Both of us got quiet.

"Tommy," I said, mostly because I hate silence more than almost anything, "are you called to be at the mission? You know, does God want you there?"

"I don't know. I don't."

"I think you need to figure that out, man."

"I know I do, but at the moment, I feel so lost about what I should do. It's like I can't hear God or something."

It was rather easy for me to suggest that he needed to figure out his calling; I wasn't the one who would have to live in the aftermath of whatever his decision ended up being. But I also had a sincere desire for my friend to be free. While a good portion of his early story had happened at that camp and among people who certainly loved him, Tommy's view of following Jesus today differed a great deal from those who worked alongside of him at the mission. To be honest, a part of me was kind of surprised that the boy hadn't been shot already for his differences. For instance, because he believes that his passion and love belong to God alone, Tommy refuses to say the Pledge of Allegiance—an act that might be heralded by some people who live in places like New York or California, but not in Eastern Kentucky.

It's an odd place to live, but sometimes I think the *lost* moments in life force us to consider our lives. They push us into places and realities that we all too often avoid. That's what it did for Tommy. I'll never forget the day when he called me and told me he was leaving the mission. I was shocked. Of course, I knew that he and Angie had been praying about it, but to be honest, after nearly a year of talking about this with him, I didn't think he had it in him to leave. But he did. It took time. And it wasn't without controversy and hardship. But he did it. Recently, we talked about how that decision has affected his life.

"Tommy, what ultimately was the deciding factor for you in leaving the mission?" I asked.

"I had to stop fighting God," he said. "I could no longer go to work and pretend that was where I was called to be. I think a part of me *wanted* so badly to be called to work there because it was a safe place. Sometimes I hated the safeness of it, but I was also attached to it. You know what I mean? Working there was easy. Yeah, sure, I was depressed, but sometimes battling depression is easier than facing your own demons. And for a long time I didn't want to live with the consequences of failing people or feeling like I was letting people down. But ultimately, I had to come to grips with what God wanted for me and not what everybody else wanted for me. But I wouldn't trade the experience of walking through that time. In the end, I think I'm closer to figuring things out because of feeling lost and not in spite of it."

My Questions for You

1. Can you relate to Tommy's story? How?

2. Have you ever been stuck in a situation that you felt controlled you?

Recently, I was at a coffeehouse on one of the neo-cool streets in Nashville's midtown district, and because my bank account had about thirty-two dollars in it, I was drinking tap water. I was meeting a friend there, and she was late. When Cassie finally arrived, we ended up chatting about her life.

"What have you been up to?" I asked, taking a sip of my ice water.

"You know, Matthew, life is going really well at the moment; I feel like I am living a little life for the first time in three years," she said, smiling from ear to ear.

"Really? What's happened?" I asked, knowing that she'd been looking for a *real* job and a *good* husband since 1998.

"That's just it," she said, "nothing really to speak of has happened to me. I still don't have a job that I am passionate about, and I am still *very* single, but I just decided that I wasn't going to let the disappointments of life get in the way of living. While my circumstances haven't changed, I'm learning to believe that *waiting* on God doesn't mean I'm not supposed to not enjoy my life. I can still be happy or at least content."

"That's kind of exciting, Cassie!" I said. "That's a very positive outlook, especially coming from you." We laughed. "But what about your writing career? Are you still pursuing that?"

"Of course! I've not stopped pushing forward with my writing," said Cassie. "But you know how that is: My dream of writing follows me, which, come to think of it is kind of like my psycho ex-boyfriends. And sometimes *my dream* is just about as healthy. But yeah, I'm still working at it."

"So, do you mind me asking you something? What brought on this new perspective?"

"You want me to be honest?"

"Um, yeah, of course."

"Lots of therapy, Matthew, which helped me become comfortable with myself and also allowed me to be honest. It's a difficult process to work through your own baggage. But I've learned that sometimes it takes work to enjoy life. And that's especially true when life isn't exactly going the way you hoped. But I realized that I needed some help working through all of that. It wasn't easy, but I'm a much happier person because I started taking one day at a time and living it instead of waiting around for some magical event to occur, which as you probably know, may very well never happen."

Cassie's right; sometimes we do have to work at being curious. And sometimes, being curious is about learning how to be happy despite the circumstances that we are going through. Believe it or not, it is possible to be happy and content even when you have a dead-end job or when life seems to not be turning out like you'd planned. But you have to *live* happiness; you can't depend on your circumstances to deliver it to you.

My Questions for You

1. What is your current method of dealing with disappointing circumstances?

2. Could you be happy if those circumstances didn't change?

The Action of Waiting

One of the greatest honors of my writing career was meeting Dr. Henry Blackaby. In *Beatitude: Relearning Jesus Through Truth, Contradiction, and a Folded Dollar Bill,* a book I wrote a couple of years ago, I described my meeting with him to be like meeting Moses. Now, he didn't bang ten laws down in front of me, but there was something very alive about that eightysomething. "I think people do too much waiting on God," the author of the well-known *Experiencing God* said to me when I interviewed him. "I believe God is waiting around on us to just join him in the story he's writing. Waiting isn't about sitting around and doing nothing. God expects us to do something."

A lot has been said about the concept of *waiting* on God. And it's no secret that waiting on God is complicated. But I think in today's pop evangelical culture with all of our "if you can dream, you can do it" handbooks, God-waiting is very much misunderstood, misinterpreted, and miscommunicated.

Sometimes I think Christians often consider waiting on God equivalent to waiting in line at the DMV. (And I'm convinced that waiting in line at the DMV is what hell must be like.) We hate waiting. And I suppose since places like McDonald's and Wendy's strive to have us through their drive-through lines in less than sixty seconds, a part of us believes God should do the same. We think he may need a little help on his time-management skills. I tend to believe that happens because we instantly assume that waiting on God has something to do with our human idea of "time." I know that has often been true for me. I far too often view waiting on God as an interruption to my life rather than a mind-set that could be helpful or ultimately play a role in making me more spiritually minded.

But the truth is, waiting on God is perhaps one of the most important and significant spiritual disciplines that a follower of Jesus can pursue. Waiting equals seeking. Waiting equals serving. Waiting equals surrender. Waiting on God is a holy engagement of the life that we are presently experiencing; it's a here and now journey that asks us to become selflessly consumed with our environment. I think waiting on God is a constant reality; it's not simply a hurdle we have to jump or a requirement we have to pass.

But that kind of waiting is difficult to pull off when disappointment or frustration hits you like a ton of bricks. When life takes an unexpected turn, you sometimes have to live a lot of life before you can pull yourself together enough to even begin to *wait* on God.

I'm sure that each of us has plans for our lives—ones that we hope are set in stone. I wanted to work in the music business when I got out of college. Cassie wants to be married and have a career in writing. Learning how to *wait* through those kinds of experiences is far from easy.

Whether those plans involve the normal ones that most of us desire—falling in love, a job that will pay the bills, and two well-behaved kids—or those that are individually unique to our own life, each of us has a road map of sorts in our heads that we hope will take us exactly where we want to go. But as most of us know (from personal experience, perhaps), life doesn't usually work that way. Sometimes we mess it up with our mistakes. Sometimes "luck" just doesn't seem to be in our corner. Sometimes we blame our realities on God, and in certain instances, maybe it is his doing. And sometimes we just aren't "made" to live the life that we had planned.

I met my onetime roommate Lee Steffen when he became the art director at *CCM*. When he took the job at the magazine, he had just finished his MBA at the University of Illinois and was looking for a place to work where he could utilize both his business expertise as well as his degree in art design. But even with all of his education and design talent, Lee's heart was music, specifically, praise and worship music.

"If I could spend my life making music that celebrates and worships God, I think I'd be a happy man," I remember him saying to me more than once. Lee has always had such a heart for worshipping God; it seems to be such an integral part of who he is as a Christian. Many times, Lee would spend his evenings locked away inside his room playing his keyboard and worshipping his Creator. With as much love and passion as Lee has for God, I would have thought that the Almighty would have wanted that boy to be making music full time by now. But so far, that hasn't happened.

"Does it frustrate you that you're still not doing what you've always felt like you were called to do?" I asked Lee, who now owns his own business doing photography and graphic design.

"Yeah, bro, it is frustrating," he said with a sad glimmer in his eye. "I have tried my hardest to seek God and do my best to be faithful to what I believe he desires for my life, and so yeah, now I'm thirty years old, and I don't feel like I have gotten any closer to doing what I feel called to do. But the thing is, I am indeed closer to God. While I don't make praise and worship music for a living, I still do make it, and somehow I believe the music I make is better because of my experiences. And I'm better because I learned what it means to wait. So, in a way, I am doing it for a living."

I got some unwelcomed news in June of 2007. That was the month I learned one of my publishers pulled the plug on a project that I had worked on for nearly eighteen months. But it wasn't just the time that I had invested into this particular project that I was lamenting; it was also the emotional and mental anguish that I went through to put some of what I had written down on paper. That project was/is still very near and dear to my heart. When I got the news, on the outside I tried to keep it together—you know, remained polite and tried to be positive—but inside I was falling apart. And not to mention, the financial ramifications of not getting paid only aggravated an already bumpy beginning to my summer. For seven weeks my emotions were like a roller coaster as I began to *wait*—the sitting in the waiting room kind of wait—upon God to make everything better.

Disappointment and frustration so often cause me to focus on *me*. I'm sure you know what that feels like. Instead of engaging the life that God has put around me and in front of me, I get this overwhelming anxiety and worry in my gut about the stuff I cannot control. It's a type of nervousness that doesn't easily go away. It tends to make me want to gather my personal baggage and retreat back into a corner and feel sorry for myself and push the people I know and love away from me. And you know what? Sometimes that feels like the right thing to do because I think that's a part of the waiting process. Waiting isn't fake happiness. It's not something I can just put on and wear around the house. It's holistic. Because waiting is a contact sport. It's interaction between you and the God of the universe. Some days it's a wrestling match, like the story of Jacob in Genesis wrestling with God. Other days it's being still, like King David spending time meditating, playing the harp, and writing poetry.

I'm still learning how to be free enough to do both.

HOKEY MOMENT

Think about a biblical story where God taught someone the *action* of waiting.

a change will do you good

It is always the simple things that change our lives. And these things never happen when you are looking for them to happen. Life will reveal answers at the pace life wishes to do so. You feel like running, but life is on a stroll. This is how God does things.

—DONALD MILLER

Change: Hate It. Need It.

Nothing bucks your ability to be curious about life like a little change. Of course, life changing is inevitable. This is true no matter who you are. Life is constantly surprising us with a various array of changes. Some of these changes are welcomed. Others are not. But either way, we have to learn to make the best of the happenings—good and bad— that occur in our lives. And therein lies the potential problem: Sometimes we try to run from change. Or we try to outfox it or pretend it isn't happening. But change still happens whether we adjust to it or not.

A couple of my friends have started reminding me that I'm nearing middle age. I hate them for reminding me of that fact. The most annoying part is the tone they use—one that makes me think they truly believe they are being helpful. But they're right, I guess. The last time November 18 rolled around, I turned thirty-four. But I must say that, so far, I've thoroughly enjoyed my thirties. For me, it has been far better than being twentysomething. I feel more comfortable in my own skin. I'm free to ask questions. Big ones. Small ones. And I'm also okay with other people having answers to some of those questions without feeling like I have to challenge them or arrive at their conclusion. And I'm finally realizing that I won't ever have all of the answers. I don't think these epiphanies are a direct result of being in my thirties, but I do believe that age, experience, and maturity can give us a little peace of mind if we allow them to. But like most changes, aging also has its share of challenges.

Now, as you might assume, there's nothing too spectacular about turning thirty-four. I mean, it's not like you expect a huge party, and you probably wouldn't take it personally if your mother accidentally forgets to send you a card with money. To me, it's kind of like turning twenty-seven or forty-two. No frills are needed—the perfect celebration requires only a couple of good friends, a good bottle of something you like, and Imogen Heap playing in the background. However, I suppose the one thing for me that has been very interesting about turning thirty-four is that I'm frighteningly close to being considered middle-aged and another year closer to dying. I'll admit; I'm a little anxious about becoming middle-aged. I think that's normal.

Entering a new season of life requires getting comfortable with a little age-inflicted change and sometimes that's difficult, even though I've always prided myself in being an advocate for change. In fact, I'm usually the first person to help many of my friends see the value in being okay with God making a few adjustments to their lives. It's easy, really; I just sit and listen to their bleeding hearts and then I encourage them to lean into the change. I say clichés. "This too will pass," I've said on so many occasions. It's funny how easy change can be when you're not the one experiencing it.

"Always remember what Sheryl Crow says," I told one friend, who was prepping to have to break up with a boyfriend, "I think a change will do you good." I then proceeded to sing it for her. She stopped me when I started doing the background vocals.

But isn't that what we've always thought friends are supposed to do? You know how it is; we pretty much lie through our teeth about how easy change is. With a few flowery sentences we try to make it sound easy, enjoyable even. If we're really good, we try to work in one or two informative references about how God is going to be there for them. I have no problem with a little change when it's happening to or affecting other people. In fact, I almost enjoy it. I like it when other people come to me for advice. I like feeling needed. I've walked with friends as they've experienced everything from a divorce to a move across the country to a change of career to a new fashion statement. I can handle all of their changes just fine, with a confident yet sometimes annoyingly perfect grace that no doubt irks people at times.

But everything changes when "change" becomes personal. I become an utter hypocrite in fact. I don't always understand why, but everything seems to become scary. I forget the advice I so quickly offer friends. In fact, it's difficult even hearing it (or rehearing it). I start to question what I've known to be true most of my life. I fear. I become anxious. I allow my thoughts to consume me to such a degree that I'm hardly any fun to have around.

But do you want to know what's weird about change? Oddly enough, all of those personal vendettas that I feel toward change don't stop me from craving it. Yes, I crave it.

I suppose this is true for a lot of us. Sometimes change is exciting to experience. It gives us something to look forward to, a new adventure to encounter. Sometimes change puts us in a new geography, a new relationship, a new job, or in a new place in life. And while we often crave those situations, we also fear them, because it often makes us grow up, give up, let go.

And believe it or not, that's a good thing.

My Questions for You

1. In what ways does change scare you?

2. How does change inspire you?

3. If you could change one thing about your life right now, what would it be?

God and Change

In my little corner of the world, many of the conversations I have with friends and family are about how we want to change something. I can't tell you how many times a bunch of us get together at coffeehouses and sit around with our cool little Mac Books, and while trying to use important words, wax philosophical about how we'd like to change things like the war in Iraq, Lindsey Lohan's catastrophic career choices, the AIDS epidemic in Africa, the environment pretty much everywhere, the colors of the paint on our walls, and the wardrobes of Paula Abdul and Katie Couric. And as varied as these topics might seem, it's not uncommon for us to talk about them as though they're all connected somehow—as if changing one could possibly create a domino effect and change the world.

But you know, I tend to think it's easy to desire change when we think we're in control. It's not nearly as scary when we think we can play God.

Like any normal person, I want change to happen on my terms, which means I want to experience it gradually, have psychiatric help available to me, and make sure I have a foolproof exit strategy. See? *Playing God.* But rather than playing his role, God asks us to trust him in the middle of change, whether that change is brought on by our own decisions or whether it catches us completely off guard.

It's not easy to trust, because our perspective of God is tainted. Because we change, our circumstances change, and the people in or lives change, we assume he will. Author Brennan Manning is like a present-day prophet to me. Though I'm sure he wouldn't consider himself anything closely resembling a prophet, I believe his words about the love of God are some of the most powerful and life giving in my lifetime. I like what he has to say about God's consistency. In his book *The Ragamuffin Gospel*, Brennan writes, "[God] is not moody or capricious; He knows no seasons of change. He has a single relentless stance toward us: He loves us. He is the only God man has ever heard of who loves sinners. False gods—the gods of human manufacturing—despise sinners, but the Father of Jesus loves all, no matter what they do" (Multnomah 2005).

How often do you think of God as this mean-spirited being that only wants to do harm in your life? I know that I've certainly looked at God in that way. Instead of having faith in God, I fear him. I don't trust him enough to even take the first step. I assume he is going to abandon me. But that isn't God. That's an idea of God I've formed because of my past experience, my brokenness.

Of course, knowing that God is consistent—that he isn't moody—still doesn't make change easy. But it does give us something to hold onto in the midst of the chaos; it does make us feel slightly less psychotic. When you know that there is something/someone consistently loving you and cheering you on and excited by your journey, the process of experiencing change is made much simpler. When I set my heart and mind on the fact that God wants nothing more than for me to succeed, grow, learn, and be passionate, I eventually find some peace in the middle of change. It's a difficult journey at times, but it's in these times that I must remember this: God isn't about making difficult circumstances more difficult. Sure, it might seem that way at times. But that's not God's style. He's about making things good. Not easy. Not better. Not perfect. But good. I tend to think of him as a larger-than-I-can-imagine force that is constantly in the process of redeeming our stories, bringing our lives back to the places where security isn't necessarily promised, but is revealed. I believe whatever circumstances I enter, God works to get me into *waiting* position, and he tends to do that whether I want him to or not.

But sometimes I go kicking and screaming, which I don't think is always a bad thing.

I met Johnny at a church on the outskirts of St. Louis. As we sat in comfy chairs and talked about some of the good and hardships of life, the arms and legs of my new friend shook rather consistently. The entire time we chatted, Johnny's body never stopped moving. His movements were unplanned, unrehearsed, and unrelenting. Almost twenty years ago Johnny had been diagnosed with Parkinson's disease, a condition that slowly steals away one's basic functionalities.

"It was a huge blow when I found out," Johnny said to me. "But there was this part of me—a small part—that said, 'Oh well, I'm not sure what God's going to do with this one, but I'm going to try and make the best of it.' But when something that's happening in your life is breaking other people's hearts and testing other people's faith, making the best of it is most definitely a process. But it's a process you have to work through, whether you planned it or not."

The way people talked about Johnny, you would think he was an angel. "He's one of the most encouraging men I've ever met," said one of the churchgoers. "He's real, sensitive, and loves God." And after meeting him, I'm not convinced that he isn't an angel.

In addition to being a good soul, Johnny is probably best known for his musical prodigy. In the early 1980s, he played in a band that traveled around the country gigging at colleges, churches, bars, and any place else that welcomed them. His first instrument was the piano.

"Matthew, I think that was the most difficult part of this whole thing for me," he said, "losing my ability to play the piano. I think a part of me believed that I would never lose that. It was mind-blowing. Playing the keys was how I communicated with God. I found so much joy in playing. When I lost that, I became depressed for a time. I'm pretty sure that the day I realized I couldn't play any longer will be etched in my brain for the rest of my life. It was such a low point. But you know what? I've discovered a whole lot of grace in the changes that I've experienced over the years."

"I'm sure you have," I smiled, "Can you talk to me about the grace?"

"Oh, the grace I've encountered far outweighs the pain. Sometimes it's just difficult to get to a place where you can see it. For one, having Parkinson's has given me the ability to relate to those who are sick. I can't tell you how many times someone will come up and talk to me about some of their deepest problems. I guess, because of what I have, people trust me with their stories of pain and sickness and other things. I get invited to pray over the sick. It has given me countless chances to talk about my faith with people, even strangers. And also, it has opened up an opportunity for me to teach Bible here at the church. I love studying Scriptures. And so, I've learned through grace and walking as closely as I can to God that change isn't fun, but I can make the most out of it."

"For someone who is facing change in their life, what advice do you have, Johnny?"

"Trust," he said. "It may sound like an easy answer to some and perhaps trite to others. But it's so true. We as people of faith must trust in God to make things good. And I'm not talking about good from our perspective, but good from his perspective. That takes work and prayer and growing, but it's possible. I've seen it in my life."

Whether we like it or not, we all experience change. Sometimes, like Johnny's experience, that change is traumatic and propels us into circumstances we would have never imagined, and sometimes change is just a part of life and reflects experiences we all go through.

My Questions for You

1. How is God a part of the changes that you experience in this life?

2. Have you ever viewed him as a part of the problem?

3. Does it comfort you to know that God is unchanging?

Getting Older, Experiencing Change

I'll be the first to admit that I'm a seriously nosey person at times. Oh, sadly, it's true. My wife constantly has to remind me not to stare at people. I don't mean to do it; it's just that sometimes I go into a trance and hardly know it's happening. I suppose my subconscious is just fascinated with people watching. I like to watch how "change" happens in the lives of my older, more experienced friends.

I learn a lot by watching my friends experience change. Sometimes their experiences are informative, while other times they are entertaining—kind of like watching a comedy. I like listening in when they're getting honest about what part of the change they're struggling through. And it's not all about just hearing about their screwups. I mean, while I've always heard that I should do my best to learn from other people's stupidity, my quest to be nosey is much deeper than just avoiding my friends' mistakes. I want to hear other people's stories so I have an idea about how life will be down the road. *What are their biggest frustrations? What do they value most?*

Whom should I talk to about creating a will? Those are the things that I want to know.

But as I get ready to hit "middle age," I've been watching my friends, and I think a couple of them are experiencing a little bit of a midlife crisis. Wayne, a guy I know from college, seems to be the worst. Out of the blue one day as we sat around with our oversweetened coffee drinks, he started talking about the early '90s like they were the good ole days. Seriously. His wife says he's begun forcing their eight-year-old to wear flannel shirts and black combat boots. And poor Wayne has once again begun slicking his hair back with what I can only suppose is L.A. Looks hair gel—the green kind for extra hold, of course. While he hasn't bought a motorcycle or tried out for any sports that require jock straps, it's still a bit uneasy for me to see him in this condition.

"Dude, I pulled out that first Pearl Jam CD the other day," he said to me recently; he then proceeded to raise both of his arms up in the air and contorted his hands into "devils," which I honestly think might be the international symbol for "loser." "I always knew that band rocked, but I had forgotten how much, bro! Dang, it's a good album. Makes me miss college, you know?"

Prior to seeing a few of my friends partying like it's 1992, I had been under the impression that, if any segment of the population could make the midlife crisis seem en vogue, it would be Generation X. *My generation.* Most of us in the Gen-X category are quite proud of our generational name; it's a pop-cultural moniker that we tend to rub in the faces of those who are not Gen-X, usually because we're totally convinced that they want to be a part of Gen-X, too. And perhaps we have a right to think that; I mean, we *are* the original fans of Nirvana, a band that convinced us that good music didn't exist until 1990. And too, we know that shows like *Grey's Anatomy* wouldn't have had a chance unless we had watched *Melrose Place* and given Heather Locklear's career a second birth. True Gen-Xers also know that the first three seasons of MTV's *Real World* is the only true reality TV.

In his book *Sex, Drugs, and Cocoa Puffs,* pop-cultural writer/author Chuck Klosterman wrote, "[A friend wrote to me and said,] you know how historians call people who came of age during World War II 'the greatest generation'? No one will ever say that about [Generation X]; we'll be 'the cool generation.' That's all we're good at, and that's all you and your friends seem to aspire to" (Scribner 2004, 43).

Though I kind of hate admitting it, Klosterman's friend is right. But it might be even worse than what he thought; sometimes I wonder if we're the only ones who actually call ourselves cool—that it's a figment of our imaginations. Hmm. Now, don't get me wrong; every generation has its issues, but mine seems to suffer from an incessant need to be cool and relevant, which to me seems like little more than a resistance toward growing up. Sure, my friends might simply be feeling a little displaced nostalgia for the pop-cultural fare of their youth or maybe they really are experiencing a crisis of sorts—a flood of disappointment as a result of rethinking their lives up to this point. I don't believe I've ever reached the halfway point of anything without becoming a little depressed or anxious or self-aware, mostly because I want to know whether or not I'm wasting my time or concentrating on the wrong things or slipping behind the rest of the pack or if I should scrap the project altogether. Anytime you're halfway through something, things might actually get difficult, but I don't think they have to be, not if you're willing to grow up.

I have met quite a few people in my life who don't seem able to grow up.

I met twenty-six-year-old Catherine when she applied to work at a coffeehouse that I managed while living in Northern Virginia. When she walked in to interview for one of the open barista positions, she was dressed just shy of fashionable, like a JC Penney mannequin. Catherine seemed confident, kind of like a model seems secure. She sat down in the chair across from mine, crossed her legs, and spoke to me in a fake British dialect.

"I need you to know one thing right off the bat," she said, smoothing the wrinkles out of her pinstripe suit with her hand, "this is not a career position for me. I probably won't be working here for too long."

"Okay," I said, a little taken back by her forthrightness. Of course, she didn't have to tell me that; I was well aware that a job at Jammin' Java, a Christian coffeehouse that paid baristas $6.50 an hour, wasn't going to be her career. In fact, I'm pretty certain I knew that better than she did, since I wasn't the one who showed up for the interview wearing three-inch stiletto heels.

"I'm an actress and a model," she said with a kind of seriousness usually reserved for jobs that require degrees in economics or physics. "I feel like I've been called to be a Christian Julia Roberts. I want to eventually do fun romantic comedies."

"Wow," I said, unaware that I was talking to God's pretty woman, "that's a lofty goal, Catherine. So, why in the world are you living in Vienna, Virginia?"

"Well, I'm still living at home. Living with Mom and Dad is a lot cheaper than a one-room flat in New York City!" she said in a much less serious tone and losing her fake British dialect.

"Are you saving up for a move?" I asked.

"Well, my plans are a little up in the air at the moment. Let's just say that life has been a little bit crazy of late. A year ago I finished my graduate degree in teaching, but I'm *so* not cut out to be a teacher. I tried it for a year, and it almost killed me. I've finally decided to pursue my dream of acting."

"Have you done any acting?" I asked.

"Only a couple things here and there," she said. "Mostly back in high school. But I loved it!"

I think about Catherine quite often. As far as I know, she never did become an actress. But she was always thinking about it. Unfortunately, there was always something a little sad about her, an insecure demeanor that wouldn't allow her to grow up. When she was twenty-six, she was making life decisions that a lot of nineteen-year-olds have already made. Though she had (and I'm assuming, still has) dreams, she always seemed to fear making the decisions that would get her there. She always had an excuse. She blamed her parents for encouraging her to get a teaching degree. She blamed God for never giving her a chance. She blamed lovers for getting in the way. The last time I heard from Catherine she was still living with her mom and dad in Northern Virginia; she was thirty-one years old and preparing to go into the army. When we talked, she smirked when she said, "Yeah, it's time to grow up, I suppose."

You think?

Some of the happiest people I know are those who don't mind getting old and facing the ordinary changes that life brings. I know that sounds simple, but it's so true. The people who figure out life, the ones who have the best stories to tell, are almost always those who engage the changes that life brings. They don't fight the natural process of life. At least, not too much. They pursue maturity instead of fearing it or avoiding it all together. They don't simply put on an act; they are alive.

Lindsey Brown is that kind of person to me. To most people, there would probably not be anything particularly interesting about Ms. Brown. She's a church secretary, a mother to three boys, and best known for two things: her smile and her hugs. Wouldn't it be great to be known for your smile and your hugs? I want to believe those are the types of qualities that the disciples loved about Jesus. Simple things. Human things. Things that didn't cost any money to give away.

"Oh, Matthew, I don't have any secret to share," she said when I asked Lindsey what makes her so happy. In fact, the forty-eight-year-old blushed and said, "Go ask somebody else!"

But I twisted her arm.

"Well, it's simple really; my mom and dad taught me to enjoy life!" she said, albeit reluctantly. "I grew up in a very simple home. I married my high school sweetheart when we both turned nineteen. We told each other at the very beginning that, whether we were in good times or in bad, we'd do our very best never to complicate life. Too many young people live utterly complicated lives, and I think that's so sad! When life is overwhelming, it's difficult making necessary changes. I guess my hubby and me always believed that the more 'stuff' change affected, the harder change would be to navigate through. Does that answer your question?"

"Well, can I ask one more question?"

"Shoot."

"For you, what's life about?"

"Enjoyment. I believe one of the best ways we can worship God is to enjoy life. When I learned to stop fearing what I could not control and started living each day with as much energy as the good Lord gave me, that's when I really started living."

Our stories involve a lot of change. Some of the changes we experience are the necessary kind, the stuff that requires us to grow up. Other changes we encounter are unexpected. When you're at a point in your story when you're trying to figure life out, I've found change can actually help you make a few discoveries about life. God seems to show up in strange and interesting ways when I am willing to walk through change with him. I've learned, grown, and healed when I've been willing to press into change, rather than resist it.

My Questions for You

1. What changes are you experiencing in your life right now?

2. Do you ever find yourself resisting change, rather than pressing into it?

sometimes truth hurts

God offers to every mind its choice between truth and repose.
Take which you please—you can never have both.

—RALPH WALDO EMERSON

The *Truth (Puke)*

"You're seriously starting to freak me out, Matthew!" said Stephanie, one the editors I worked with at *CCM*. "I don't know what's gotten into you, but you're acting ridiculous. I'm not talking to you right now. Just leave."

"Oh, come on, Stephanie," I griped, "I've had a difficult week; if anybody knows this, it's you. Can we please get this cleared up?"

"No, I'm not talking to you when you're like this," she said.

"Please," I said.

"Matthew!" said another one of the editors, who was about as healthy as cancer. "Just leave us alone! You're being a jerk! We need some time before we can make this right."

"Fine."

I walked out of Stephanie's office, down the hallway toward my office, and tears started filling my eyes. It had been one of the longest and most emotionally heavy weeks of my life. Only three days before, I had been told by one of the Salem publishers that a group of six

Christian music publicists that I had to work with didn't like me. The whole situation had made me extremely paranoid and angry, but Stephanie was right; I was acting like a nutcase. I had a decent excuse to be hysterical, but that didn't seem to matter.

I loved working with Stephanie. In addition to her being a great editor, you could always trust her to be frank. But since I was raised in a family that tended to sweep issues under the rug until further notice, sometimes frank was difficult for me to take. It's hard having someone hold a mirror up to your face and show you your reflection.

The truth is sometimes hard to take. Sometimes it downright hurts. There are times when the truth has shown me something painful about my abilities, my story, a lost job, or a broken relationship. Certain situations and events continue to reveal what is true about myself and about life. And sometimes this truth is hard to take.

Upon deciding to write this book, I told my editor that I didn't want to write a book that simply tells people what they want to hear. Sure, I wanted this book to be encouraging to you as you pursue your passions and engage in a curious journey, but I didn't want to avoid telling the truth, either. Unfortunately, a lot of people don't like to hear the truth, especially when it's about them personally or about the hopes and dreams they desire. In fact, every once in a while somebody will run right smack into something true, and then proceed to vomit.

I have to be honest; there was a time when I thought the whole "truth vomit" was only real by Hollywood's standards, a vividly dramatic way for makers of a must-see drama to demonstrate that a character has seen some kind of light. Or darkness. Think about how many of the bad guys on *Law & Order SVU* end up heaving up their last meal after being interrogated by Christopher Meloni. That guy could bring the truth out of the pope. How about actress Maria Bello's famous puking scene in the 2005 movie *History of Violence*? Here we have a woman who knows her husband killed two men in a diner, witnessed him brutally smash some guy's nose in through his skull, and again watched him kill two others in her front yard—but umm, *no puking*. Maria even endures bruise-inducing sex with her husband, and again, no puking. However, when she learns the truth about her husband's involvement in the mob—*yep*—that's when she pukes.

For some reason, God has hardwired some people's stomachs to react chaotically when something true hits for the first time. For some people, truth is like ipecac, the syrupy goo that will save your life if you accidentally swallow rat poison, but will do it by way of upchucking. Which means you still may break out in a cold sweat, shake hysterically, vomit, and then pass out, but the ultimate result—death versus life—is extraordinarily different.

As difficult as it is to take, that's why truth is good. If we will heed its warning or advice, it sometimes saves us. Of course, sometimes it doesn't *feel* like it's saving us. However, even when truth is making us feel like we're losing everything, if we face it or own up to it, truth can also help us navigate our way through life. Like a compass, truth will save us if we follow it.

My Questions for You

1. What truth have you discovered about yourself that has been difficult to process?

2. Who are the people in your life who are willing to tell you the truth?

3. In your journey, what truth have you ignored?

The Truth Will Find You Out

Samantha Hines knows what it feels like to be bombarded by the hard truth. "Sometimes when you realize the truth and heed it, you feel like you're giving up on a dream," she said. "It's hard to swallow." The twenty-six-year-old graduated three years ago with a degree in public relations and advertising. After college, she moved to New York City with plans to work in the fashion industry. That was her goal.

"Ever since I was a little girl," she said to me, "it has been my dream to work in fashion. All along, I kind of knew that I wasn't talented enough to be a designer, so I chose a career path that would allow me to potentially work in the business side of the fashion world. I felt called to that world," she said. "For one, it's well-known for being a dark industry, one that isn't too friendly to Christians. And two, I wanted to do something that I loved, that I was passionate about, and 'helping people look their best' has always been something that has come natural to me. When I moved to New York, I had already landed an entry-level position in the advertising department at a major designer. Needless to say, I was ecstatic about the opportunity. I couldn't wait to get started.

I was twenty-three and already had my foot in the door at one of the major designers."

Though Samantha certainly knew the industry she was venturing into was cutthroat, she actually had no idea what she was getting herself into. "Matthew, it was horrible!" she yelled into the phone. "My boss was nice to me for *one* day! After that, he became like the male version of Meryl Streep in *The Devil Wears Prada*! He was evil. And I was his peon. On top of working seventy-five hours a week, most of the work I did was for his personal crap. I was setting up dates for he and his wife. I was setting up dates for he and his girlfriend too. And that's just the beginning."

"What happened?" I asked.

"Ugh!" she grunted, "I was just overworked, underpaid, and losing my sanity. And I am well-known for my sanity, Matthew! I'm a little proud of it; I had been put into difficult circumstances before, and I had always come out on top. I was determined to win against that evil man! You know what I mean? I wasn't going to let him ruin my chances to work in the industry that I'd been dreaming about since I was like ten. So I stuck it out for two years. But I couldn't do it. I had to quit."

"You quit?" I asked. "What changed your mind? What was the final straw?"

"The final straw was me really. I'd become this awful jaded person. My mother said to me on several occasions, 'Samantha, I am *not* talking to the girl that I raised! You've become someone I hardly recognize.' Oh, Matthew, I can't tell you how much that hurt. At first, I convinced myself that Mom was overreacting, but when I told my friends what was going on, they agreed with my mother.

And they never agreed with my mother! I ended up quitting because I knew that God didn't plan on me becoming some 'new Samantha,' and the new Samantha didn't care one lick about being light. I had to leave to save myself. But that was hard; I mean, I was giving up my dream. But I knew it was the right thing for me."

Here's something you might want to spend some time thinking about: Do you know your own personal limits? Let me explain: Personal limits are those boundaries that each of us should have about what we are or aren't willing to do. In other words, consider these questions: Do you work well under pressure? Can you handle a high amount of stress? Are you willing to live in a big city? Or do you prefer a smaller, quieter environment? Would you live overseas? Do you mind working with problematic people? Do you mind working with children? The list could go on.

While we should anticipate our limits being stretched from time to time, it's important for us to know ourselves well enough to gauge the probability that we will be able to function healthily in a particular working environment. Some might view "limits" as weakness, but I tend to think of them as small God-given truths that help each of us discover what will make us happy. I don't believe God ever expects us to remain on a career path that would force us to act outside of what comes natural for us. In other words, if you're naturally a creative person, I don't believe God expects you to work as an engineer. Again, that's not to say that our boundaries can't change or grow with time, but who we are at the core does not. The essence of who we are should never change because of our environment.

My Questions for You

1. How well do you know yourself? (Your personality? Your likes and dislikes? Your values?)

2. Would you be willing to change things in your life if what you were doing overstepped your personal limits?

Talent and Truth

I live in Nashville, Tennessee. Because my education is in the music business, I've always been privy to the town's "music scene." As you probably know, a lot of people who relocate to Nashville don't simply *move* here; they're called here. I've always thought that was a little strange. I mean, there's no one making random phone calls to people all over the world telling them to move to Nashville. But apparently, God really loves this town, because according to an awful lot of people who show up here with nothing but a guitar and a suitcase of clothes, he's constantly calling people and asking them to move to Music City.

As you know, Nashville is one of the mother ships for those hoping to make good on a calling. It's not *the* mother ship, but it's often the city dreamers run to when they're not quite ready to make the move to New York City or L.A. Of course, that's not always true, but it does seem like a good number of people view Music City as either a non-murderous alternative to moving to the left or right coasts or as a nice place to vacation for eight or nine years before making the big transition east or west.

The stereotypes about Nashville are true. Ninety-six percent of the people serving you at places like T.G.I. Friday's, Panera Bread, The Cheesecake Factory, or Wendy's want to be famous some day (one of the 80 percent of statistics that are completely made up on the spot). They've been dreaming about it for a long time. While carrying hot spinach artichoke dip in one hand and a couple of Bud Lights in the other, Nashville's finest servers become experts at figuring out whether or not they *need* to know you. Most aren't talented enough to sing their way through an a cappella version of "Happy Birthday" without going flat, but they can spot record producers, talent agents, or someone crazy enough to become their superfan with no trouble at all.

The stories of what brings these musical wannabes here are similar yet still unique enough to be fascinating to listen to. I've listened to a million of them. And to be honest, while I do sometimes feel sorry for some of them, I am mostly intrigued by their passionate pursuit of what they feel as though God or somebody or something has called them to do. The naïve passion of someone who wants to sing or act for a living is contagious; maybe that's why most of them sacrifice the comfort of their small hometowns, where they were considered local celebrities, to move to the city where dreams usually crash and burn, but once in a while come true.

And every one of them believe with all of their hearts that they are capable of being one of the few.

I've known a good number of people who have come to this town unaware of the reality that awaits them. I've met those who are now famous and those who are still serving at restaurants. And I know some who have hightailed it back to their hometowns, feeling defeated by the craziness of the industry. Of course, some of them survive the madness of Nashville's country or Christian music industries, and some of them get swallowed up by the drama, the frustration, or the deflation of hearing "No, I'm sorry; you're not what we're looking for."

Many of them could avoid becoming hurt by simply realizing the reality of their talent and, more importantly, recognizing the level of the talent of those who do make it in this town. But that's difficult to see when you're dreaming big, and that's even more difficult to tell somebody. And sure, theoretically, a person can get better with practice. But because I've seen a lot of crash and burn stories, I know that it's quite rare that they become good enough to "make it."

Recently, I befriended a Starbucks employee who wanted to either become a singer/songwriter or a songwriter. After I heard him sing, I realized that if he was destined to become anything in this industry, it would be a songwriter. The kid couldn't carry a tune.

"You used to be the editor at *CCM*, didn't you?" he said. I nodded my head yes and ordered a grande bold. "Would you ever be willing to listen to my music? I'm a songwriter! And I'd love to get your opinion about my songs."

I'm never sure how I should answer that question, mostly because, while I have worked in the Christian music industry, my point of view is hardly final. But I have a difficult time *not* being honest. I've been in too many workshops with people in this industry who are way too nice, unable to be upfront and honest with a person about their level of talent. While I don't ever want to discourage a person from pursuing their dreams, I also don't want to give a person so much hope that they end up moving to Nashville because they believe they have a shot. But he was a nice kid.

"Sure," I said, "but on two conditions: One, I will be very honest with you. And, two, my point of view is only that, just my point of view."

"That sounds great, man," he said, "and I totally want you to be honest with me."

A few weeks later, he came over to my home, sat in my living room, and played me some of his songs.

"What did you think?" he asked.

"Your lyrics aren't horrible, man," I said. "But you aren't planning on singing these songs, right?"

"I've got a cold," he said. "And my voice has hardly had any time to warm up. You know what I mean?"

"Do you want my honest opinion, man?" I asked.

"Yes, I do," he said, lying through his teeth.

"Bro, like I said, your songs aren't horrible. I think the melodies are pretty average and some of the lyrics don't make a lot of sense. But most of that can be fixed."

"Hmm. Do you think I have any shot at this?"

"That's not for me to decide, man. But I think it's necessary for you to figure out what role music is going to play in your life. Is it going to be a hobby that you dabble in? Or are you going to pursue it as your full-time gig? If I were you, I'd make it a hobby."

"But bro, music is my life; I can't give up on it! My wife and I moved here so I could pursue this dream, and I can't just make it a hobby."

"And like I said, that's for you to decide. If that's what you're feeling, then you need to chase it. Just remember, sometimes our talents are only meant to be hobbies or something we do on the side. And that's not giving up on your dreams. That's just realizing what might be true for you, bro."

Gosh, that kind of conversation is hard. But sometimes it's necessary. Sometimes it's freeing.

I know very well what that Starbucks employee was feeling; like him, music was my life growing up. Quite honestly, it was my saving grace. Because I couldn't play sports to save my life, I found a great deal of comfort in the fact that I could play the lead in every church musical I got my hands on. When I was younger, my voice was exceptional. I could hit notes that most women only dreamed about. And every time I sang in church or in a competition or starred in a play, something inside of me just felt at home. People were constantly telling me that my voice was wonderful. They told me I should be on *Star Search*. They told me that God was going to use my voice. However, when I moved to Nashville, eventually I had to face reality about my hopes and dreams of becoming a singer: While I was good enough to sing in church and at nursing homes, I wasn't good enough to be a recording artist. Was that difficult to swallow? Yes. But I can't tell you how grateful I am that I learned it then.

The harsh reality is this: Sometimes the stuff that we love to do or even the stuff that we're extremely talented at can't be the way we make ends meet. In other words, not all of us will become famous! Lots of people who are creative or athletic or talented in a specific area don't like to hear that. And more than you know, I can understand that. But I've had to learn that just because you're not making your living using your talent doesn't mean you are wasting it. It doesn't mean that you can't use it in another capacity. There are other ways to utilize the gifts God gives us. And sometimes, we have to search those "other ways" out. But they do exist. And it's important that we find them.

I am almost clueless when it comes to anything involving business. That's kind of sad considering I have a bachelor's degree in business administration. So, anytime I'm around someone who is talented at business, I kind of become a little envious. My friend James is one of those guys; almost anything he touches somehow turns from a huge "risk" to gold. Over the years I've tried to copy the actions of James' business practices, but for some reason, I never get the same result. But James has one big problem; he's cockier than Mike Tyson in 1991. And perhaps lucky for him, that almost ruined him.

"I was raking in about 12k a month only a couple years ago," James told me, sounding a little less certain than the last time we talked. "Life was *too* easy back then, man. I got in over my head I guess. And because I hate to quit or to lose, I ignored all of the obvious signs telling me to get out."

Nearly eight years ago, James and a buddy of his started a real estate business together. They bought fixer-uppers, renovated them, and then resold them for a rather impressive profit. "Lots of other people were doing the same thing back then, but we jumped in when the 'getting in' was good!" said James. "Dave and I couldn't believe how quickly we were able to turn a profit. It was insanely good. It almost felt like we could do no wrong."

"But eventually, it did go sour, right?"

"Heck, yeah," he said, "we got prideful or selfish or stupid— *whatever you want to call it*—and eventually, the whole business went south! I haven't spoken to Dave in nearly eighteen months other than through my lawyer. It's depressing to even think about."

"If you don't mind me asking this," I said, "have you learned anything from the experience?"

"Matthew, my story up until that point was so easy. The stuff that I loved to do, I did. I'd never experienced anything close to that in my life. Sure, I had drama in my life, but I was able to control it. When I lost control of my business and lost a friendship in the process, I almost went crazy. In fact, I did go to see a shrink to help me get through all of this stuff. And so, yeah, I learned some hard lessons from all of that stuff, but embracing the truth from that kind of experience is a process, and one that doesn't come easy."

For each of us, truth comes in many shapes and sizes. Sometimes it's as obvious as the fat man who is blocking a perfect view. Other times it takes a few moments (or days or years) to sink in. And at times it's a huge surprise that you aren't prepared to hear. Truth is a chameleon of sorts; it can take on the likeness of the IRS, a broken leg, or a bathroom scale. Sometimes it brings discomforting news. It might scream: "For goodness sake, would you please shut up?" when everyone is tired of hearing you talk. Or "You're making a fool of yourself," when you're trying to act cooler than you really are. Or "Just because Aunt Dorothy says you can sing doesn't mean you're the next Kelly Clarkson," when you're about to move to Nashville. Truth is all around us. It might come by way of a friend, your mom or dad, an employer, a professor, a preacher, or Tony Bennett.

But no matter what kind of truth comes into one's life, it doesn't have to be the kind that kills your dream. It might alter how you view your dream, but you shouldn't let it die.

As you hopefully know, this truth doesn't come only from Bible studies or preachers. It might come as a spirited reminder that nobody likes a jerk (and that you're being one)! It might be the voice of reason, the one that's telling you to think or to not move so quickly or to stop doing something all together.

Okay, so what would happen if we began listening to these little truths that come our way? What if we listened to the stories that happen in our lives? What if we began to let the stories teach us something about ourselves? In my personal life, I have experienced over and over again moments when I'm convinced that God is speaking to me within my own personal narrative. It isn't always through a burning-bush type of sign; sometimes it's just an experience that pushes me toward the curious path I am called to experience.

Of course, unfortunately, like I wrote earlier, it's normally not much fun when we're forced to see our own reflections, especially when somebody else, or worse, *God*, is holding the mirror in front of our faces. I imagine it feels similar to being naked in a crowd of people, and of course, everyone else is usually clothed in their Sunday best. But if we seek out the simple truths that are around us, even though they're not always what we want to hear, they will save us.

My Questions for You

1. What is currently happening in your life that is teaching you something about who you are?

2. When you experience difficult circumstances, how do you normally react?

3. Can you think of a time in your life, when you've had to learn a painful truth about yourself?

God paints (and we are his art)

Success is to be measured not so much by the position that one has reached in life as by the obstacles which he has overcome.

—BOOKER T. WASHINGTON

You (the Story)

Most of us think about our stories on a regular basis. In fact, it has probably been that way since we were children when we'd spend long hours dreaming about what we would be when we grew up. I don't believe that's accidental; we dream about our lives for a purpose. Yes, believe it or not there is rhyme and reason to all of the madness. But as we get older, real life cannot only frustrate us, it can also leave us feeling jaded about who we are and what we are called to be.

Maybe that's why those who remain curious do something extraordinary or at least something they love to do. When we are curious about what God has for us, we dive into the mystery of what God desires for us to do. As I've said before, there's no secret formula for that; it's a journey, a process that doesn't end with the perfect job or the perfect relationship or the perfect dream come true. This journey we're on is constant—one that takes a lifetime to accomplish.

Too often, so many of the people I know stop the journey far too soon. They get to a place in their lives where they simply feel they've "made it" and then they stop being curious. I know people who let hard circumstances or successes make them think that there's no longer a need to remain curious about anything. Sometimes they believe they've experienced all that there is to experience. Other times they believe their dreams are dead.

I think we've all experienced those thoughts before. Sometimes, we let these kinds of thoughts control our lives. The truth is, we complicate life. We complicate God. So many of us want to process life with an acronym. Perhaps something like GOD—Get a plan. Over analyze the plan. Direct others to live by your plan.

So many of us just need to get free from all of the cliché Christian advice that we've been subject to for years and begin living life the way God intended: by faith. Did Abraham have an evangelical preacher whispering in his ear about how to live? *No.* In fact, the man didn't even have the Bible. He lived by faith, which included mistakes, miracles, celebrations, disappointments, and despite all of that, his calling was fulfilled. *How did he do that?* He was free. He was curious about God's path for him. And he followed it the best way he could. And because Abraham was curious, and because God works in the lives of his people, God painted a picture using Abraham's life. And I believe it was a work of art.

You (the Art)

I hate group discussions that involve the topics Peter Jackson or The Lord of the Rings trilogy, so whenever I am around a conversation involving either of these topics I tend to walk away, scream child-appropriate obscenities, or close my eyes and imagine myself as a famous break-dancer. I hate them because if you *like* LOTR, you're often a bit freakish about it. And if you don't like LOTR, you're a jerk about it. Put those two kinds of people in the same room in the same discussion and it can get ugly.

Several years ago, I was at a friend's house when somebody suggested we watch *The Fellowship of the Rings*. That's when it started.

"I can't believe that you, of all people, like Lord of the Rings, Matthew!" That's what my friend Samuel proclaimed after I naïvely shared my thoughts about being mesmerized with Peter Jackson's attention to detail in the scenes portraying the Shire. I was wrong to assume that everyone would appreciate the knowledge I had gleaned from watching the hours of DVD extras.

"Oh my gosh, anybody who doesn't like Lord of the Rings is an idiot," said Lisa in my defense. "Did you go to college, Samuel?"

"Did I go to college? What does my education have to do with my dislike of Lord of the Rings?" asked Sam in retaliation.

"Because I think there's a direct correlation between education and a person's ability to truly understand the soul of Tolkien's story," said Lisa.

My friend Lisa is oddly intelligent, but that's why I love her. If I ever have the opportunity, I will give her the "Anne of Green Gables" award because she quotes poetry and literature like she should have been born in 1827. She's far more obsessed with Lord of the Rings than I am; she actually read the books.

"I'm not trying to be insulting; Tolkien is hard reading for some," said Lisa. "Some of his passages are thick and difficult."

When she stopped talking, Lisa looked off into the distance as if she were alone on a huge Broadway stage and recited word for word three paragraphs from Lord of the Rings. No one needed to check and see if she was accurate; the words she enunciated with near perfect diction sounded exactly like something Bilbo Baggins would say.

"Oh, come on, Lisa; don't you think you're just a tad bit freakish when it comes to Tolkien?" asked Shawn, who is an engineer too smart for his own good, and consequently, too logically minded to ever see that as a problem. "I mean, you'd probably sleep with a Frodo doll if they existed. And you know, let's face it," he smirked, "that might be why you're still single."

Sam started laughing hysterically while attempting to give Shawn a high-five. Lisa just glared at Shawn and began mumbling something G. K. Chesterton–ish under her breath.

"We're talking about a movie, guys!" interrupted Louise, who at the time was a recovering youth pastor. "It's *just* a movie. Entertainment. It's meant to be objective. You can't judge somebody solely based on their opinions about a movie, especially Lord of the Rings."

Art Is Complicated

Throughout my life, I've found art to be complicated at times, mostly because it can bring out the extremities of our personalities, good and bad. But I've also found a lot of correlation between art and how God works in a person's life. I mean, think about it: To some degree, art is supposed to be complicated; you know, it tends to push us out of our comfort zones and make us think with colors and rhyme and beats that perhaps we would have never discovered (or even fathomed) had someone or something not put them in front of us. Doesn't God do the same things in our lives—gets us outside of what is natural for us to do? And just like we aren't always comfortable with the places that art pushes us to, we aren't always comfortable when God takes us to these places.

Much like the stories we read about in the Bible, we find pieces of ourselves within art. This is why art can resonate so deeply within our souls. The connections we feel to the stories that God and artists create hit us where we're often the most vulnerable. I believe that God is an artist. My friend Devon helped me come to this conclusion. I know Devon from my days at Jammin' Java. He worked in the guitar shop that was adjacent to the coffeehouse. Devon is one of those people who seems to be cooler than the rest of us. In fact, sometimes his suave was a detriment of sorts, mostly because a lot of people found it difficult relating to him, even if they wanted to. Women swooned around Devon, talking endlessly about how good he smelled—a mixture of *Joop!* cologne and clove cigarettes. The ladies who wanted to get to know Devon were usually attracted to his somewhat dark personality, a weird but interesting combo of innocence and bad-boy attitude. There was definitely an odd likable charm about him, one that screamed "look at me" and "save me" all at the same time. When the ordinary person looked at Devon's life from the outside, they probably thought he had it made, and there were probably a lot of people who wished they could somehow be a little more like him.

"There's just something sexy about him," said one girl, like she was in some kind of trance. "He just, I don't know, is beautiful to me."

In addition to Devon being cool, he was also a prodigy. The boy could play fifteen different instruments and, if he wanted to, he could pick another one up and know how to use it in a few hours. That's probably why most people envied him.

Devon and I became close. It's always interesting how different a person becomes when you hear the whole story. I reconnected with Devon recently, and we talked again about his life.

"Church defined me when I was a kid," Devon said, still smoking his cloves. "But back then I didn't know how to manage my demons, Matthew. In fact, I guess I kind of thought that I was actually able to 'manage' my demons."

I knew what demons he was talking about. Before I met Devon, he'd already lived a very full life. As a teenager he was diagnosed with leukemia, a rare but treatable thread of the cancer. In addition to barely living through the effects that chemotherapy had on his body, he also became clinically depressed, which pushed him into personal seclusion.

"Man, I put myself in jail," said Devon, puffing on his cigarette. "I was fifteen. I was bald. I probably needed people at that point in my life more than any other time. But I didn't want to be around people.

People thought I was making the depression up. It was horrible."

However, Devon did end up letting one person into his life, a well-known and well-loved teacher from the private school he attended. "She had battled depression too," said Devon. "And so she *got* me, which was something that I needed at the time. I needed somebody to understand just a little of what I was going through. That teacher made me believe that I had a reason to survive the cancer, and that I would eventually not feel depressed anymore, but …"

"But?" I said.

"We had an affair."

"You and the teacher? And you were fifteen?"

"Yes. At first, it was just an emotional affair—a relationship that most people just believed was a close bond between a teacher and student. But I was in love. I told her that. And she was too. And after the emotional stuff began, it became physical."

"Was there ever a time when you thought to yourself, 'This is wrong; I shouldn't be doing this'?" I asked.

"Of course."

"Why didn't you stop?"

"Matthew," he said, laughing a little bit, "do you really want me to say this for your book?"

"Yes. Just say it."

"Honestly, it felt good. And it was really nice to be loved by somebody. She didn't judge me."

"But eventually, the two of you got found out."

"Yeah, that day was horrible. That experience sent me into another battle with depression. The anxiety of feeling alone hit me again, but that time it was far worse than it was before. It was like a ton of bricks."

I wish I could say that Devon is a completely healthy person today. But I can't. I can say that he's in a much better place than before. But I can also tell you that his demons have followed him. Throughout much of his life—he's twenty-nine now—his past has always been close behind, showing up at the oddest times and stealing away his ability to enjoy life. "You know, Matthew, the church rarely teaches us how to work through guilt. We talk a lot about forgiveness, a lot about grace, but we rarely discuss how we can overcome the guilt of our pasts."

Devon stopped talking for a moment, looked up at me, and then said, "Your book is about 'figuring life out,' right?"

"Yeah, something like that," I said, giving him a half smile.

"Do you think we were ever supposed to fully figure life out?" he asked.

"No. I don't think so, at least, not completely. Life isn't simple. I think that's why so many of us are constantly longing for more, constantly searching for answers."

"Exactly," said Devon. "Some of the answers only come in time, and others won't ever be answered until we meet our Maker."

"I'm in the process of learning that I have to be *okay* with not having all of the answers," I said, "and that it's not a bad thing for there to be some mystery."

"You know, man, I'm realizing that I am God's art …"

Tears began forming in Devon's eyes.

"Oh, gosh, do you know how long it's taken me to get to a place where I can say that and mean it? A long time, bro. But I believe it now. Believe it with all of my heart. Despite all of the crap that I have caused and felt and experienced, I am God's art. And I don't think I was meant to hang in his finest of galleries. But that doesn't mean that he's stopped painting, bro. I refuse to believe that God makes ugly art. He doesn't. He makes magnificent, breathtaking art. And I'm okay with the ups and downs of my story, as long as God never stops painting my picture."

Curious People: Sholandra Black

Sholandra Black's story is inspiring to me. My interview with Sholandra focused on her dramatic childhood and her story of finding hope through very hard, difficult circumstances.

MATTHEW: Sholandra, I understand that you grew up in a pretty intense environment; can you tell me a little about that?

SHOLANDRA: Well, I guess you might be able to say that my experiences growing up were intense, that's for sure. (Laughs) I grew up in the 1980s in Harlem. My mother was a schizophrenic. And my father was a raging alcoholic. So, my home was definitely abusive, emotionally and physically. During my childhood, my mother lived in denial that Dad was an alcoholic and that he abused us. In addition to those things, I was also sexually molested when I was seven by an older childhood friend. I was a very angry teenager because of what happened to me.

MATTHEW: Wow. You've obviously been able to overcome a lot. What do you attribute that to?

SHOLANDRA: One of my mom's sisters (my aunt) was a very spiritual woman. Mom thought she was a freak, but I was always intrigued by her faith and also her certainty that each of us has a purpose in life. Somehow, she always believed that God would take care of her. When I was around sixteen, I started going to mass with my aunt. At first, I viewed it as a way of getting out of the house and away from the dysfunction of my family, but after a little bit of time, I really started listening to the words of the priest's homily. On the way home one Sunday, I asked my aunt if she thought the priest would ever meet with me to discuss some of the things that were on my mind. She was thrilled that I brought it up, and even said, "Oh, child, I've been praying that you would be open to meeting with Father Robert. He's a good soul." Matthew, that's what I did. I started having "therapy of sorts" with Father Robert once, sometimes twice, a week.

MATTHEW: Okay, so your aunt is praying for you and you're meeting with a priest, but eventually, you decided that the only thing that would save you from your life was to leave, right?

SHOLANDRA: Yes! Father Robert gave me that advice. I came in crying one day about my father's abuse toward me, and Father looked at me—and I will never forget the words he said—"Sho, sometimes God doesn't rescue us, but gives us the inside power to rescue ourselves, and when I look at you, I see that kind of inside power." Sometimes when I'm having a rough day, I have to remind myself of that inside power. (Laughs)

MATTHEW: So, what did you do next?

SHOLANDRA: I graduated from high school. Well, I should say that I barely graduated from high school. But I did. And I went to college in North Carolina. Father Robert pulled some strings and got me into a college that was close to Charlotte. The parish in Harlem even raised some funds for me to attend. I worked my butt off, and in five years, I received my MSW (Masters of Social Work).

MATTHEW: Did you seek any more counseling after leaving home?

SHOLANDRA: I did indeed. I continue to go to counseling, even now. I've always thought it was important for me to continue to work through the relational and professional issues that I encounter, mostly because I had a father who beat me and because I was sexually violated at such a young age. So many young women who have experienced similar ordeals get into lifestyle habits that make it much easier for their pasts to define who they are today. While our pasts certainly affect us, I don't believe it's God's plan for them to. I know that I am very susceptible to doing that, and so, I do counseling to help me think healthily.

MATTHEW: And you're also a counselor yourself, right? Talk to me about what you do.

SHOLANDRA: I work with young kids who have experienced life-altering circumstance such as the death of a parent, molestation, or physical abuse. I always laugh when I think about how God led me to this profession. I think so many of us find out what we are called to do professionally because of the experiences we encounter as children, good and bad. Maybe that's why they call these things "life-altering" issues, because they are. But rather than become bitter, I told God that I wanted to be happy, so do what is necessary to get me that way.

MATTHEW: Sholandra, what's your advice to the person with emotional and mental baggage resulting from their childhood but has yet to deal with it?

SHOLANDRA: Matthew, they can't walk through life alone. You need to confess to God and to yourself that you're not strong enough to handle this on your own. And then you need to go and find help. Many of the frustrations and insecurities that we deal with as children end up being the reasons we can't live healthily as adults.

What Are We Really Looking For?

God is in the business of redeeming people's stories. That's a beautiful thought, isn't it? I mean, it's comforting to know that I am incapable of making a mistake that God can't redeem. That's true for all of us. You can't out "fool" God. Like Devon said, he will always paint again, no matter how many times we mess up, screw up, or (bleep) up. Of course, I don't necessarily want to test him on that; at least, not any more than I have already.

But what are we *really* looking for out of life?

I tend to think that most of us have learned that our stories are fragile, just as we learn that glass is fragile—when it shatters. And while we try to protect ourselves from danger, we learn very quickly that we can't, that we're not in control. That truth scares us at times and invigorates us at others, but most of the time, we have to admit that we're not sure what we're supposed to think about all of it. We want to trust that God is the one who is in control, but then we turn on CNN and our theories tend to go out the window. You know what I mean? I don't believe anything messes with a person's ability to trust in God like watching the media's coverage of war.

As we get older and experience more of our story, we also become fully aware of our own *personal* humanity. In other words, we know what's really going on inside of us. While our families and friends may not know what we battle, we do. And we think to ourselves, if God can't get his hands around our fears, our addictions, or our sins, then how in the world can we believe that he's capable of taking care of our stories? That's a valid question, I believe—a question that can make faith difficult, make the Christian life difficult to live.

A lot of us have divided hearts—we fight a war between faith and logic, God and culture. The culture most of us live in teaches us that our stories aren't important. Usually, the stories that are told by the media are those of the wealthy, the intelligent, the sexy, the talented, and the revered. But if those are the only "successful" story lines, what does that mean for the majority of us? What if we can't find a job? What if we're homely or fat? What if our only "talent" is playing video games? I mean, is there a successful story line for the jobless fat guy who kicks butt at *Halo*?

It's really no wonder so many of us are investing our time and effort into "making it." Instead of living the stories that God designed us for, we settle for the generic ones—the ones advertised on TV, the Internet, and in the education systems. We buy into the "generic" stories but end up realizing—often, when we hit middle age—that the life we're living isn't the one that was advertised. We don't realize where exactly things went wrong; we just assume that the truth was somewhere in the fine print. And we didn't read it.

"I truly believe that all I was looking for was something normal," said Pamela, a thirty-eight-year-old mother of four, who lives in the suburbs of Omaha. "I married my high school sweetheart; I guess I did it because I was in love and that's what Mom did, and we're happily married, but we're hardly blown away by our lives. I feel like I'm just going through the motions, hoping for some 'lottery win' on life. But I don't have any hope of winning, mostly because you have to play to win. And Matthew, I'll be the first to admit; I don't play."

A lot of people can relate to Pamela's emotions; in fact, some of us get tired of playing when we are only twenty-three. Since we were kids, we've been told that "normal"—whatever that means—will make us happy. Most of us, at some point in our lives, have fallen for the lie that says: The "good life" comes when we have a high-paying job, a house we can call our own, a decent 401k plan, stock options, a car that doesn't embarrass us in front of our friends, a couple of kids, and a spouse who doesn't hate us. And what if we are fortunate to get everything on that list? Is there any one of us who could keep something like cancer or a drunk driver or a found-out secret from taking it all away?

Our stories were never meant to be generic. We were never meant to follow the ways of culture and pursue the easy thrills of twenty-first-century "success." While on earth Jesus talked about a higher calling. He talked about a foolish route. He said that we would know we were on the right path if it was sometimes lonely. But he also said that the "narrow path" would ultimately lead us toward spiritual fulfillment. Jesus said, "What will it profit a man if he gains the whole world, and loses his own soul?" (Mark 8:36). It wasn't a "balanced" life that Jesus talked about; it was pretty much a preposterous life. He asked his followers to scrape against the grain of the social norms—and to do it with passion, love, mercy, and forgiveness. It takes a curious soul to even consider discovering what Jesus believed life was all about.

What Life's All About

Every Tuesday and Thursday when it wasn't raining, Jerry Moreland, an eighty-six-year-old from my hometown, came into Masten Home

Center. Whenever he came into my town's local hardware store, the lady who worked with me at the cash register would follow Jerry around the store with a can of disinfectant spray. "That man smells funky!" said Janice, who was in her early fifties and had a hairdo that resembled a 1980's bouffant. "I swear that old man smells worse than a chicken coup." She was right; he didn't smell that great, but Jerry didn't have any sense of smell. So lucky for him, he never knew he smelled.

But despite his putrid scent, I loved Jerry. He was the liveliest old man I'd ever met. And in addition to being youthful and spry, the old stinky man was full of wisdom about life. "I don't believe people should retire," he said to Janice and me once. "People who retire end up dying! Why? Because they ain't got nothing to do with all of that time on their hands. I think people should work until they die!"

"That makes one of us," said Janice, who was single, bitter, and already planning her funeral. "I can't wait to retire!"

"Oh, Janice, you shouldn't do that," he warned in his thick country dialect. "And if you do, you should at least find a place to volunteer! If people retire, it should be so they can help others. Period."

"Did you retire, Mr. Moreland?" I asked.

"I retired from getting paid to work at seventy-two," the old man said with a grin. "I worked for the county's parks and recreation service for nearly fifty years! I loved every minute of it."

"And what do you do now?"

"He should have moved to Florida!" Janice said with a smirk, gripping her personal can of Lysol, waiting not so patiently to use it.

"Fiddlesticks!" said Mr. Moreland. "I wouldn't live in a retirement facility if it were the last place on earth. People weren't meant to vacation for twenty years before they die. But to answer your question, Son, my work depends on which day of the week it is."

And then Mr. Moreland listed off a slew of weekly responsibilities that included everything from doing lawn work for a couple of widows who went to his church to babysitting his grandkids to volunteering at the local jail, where he swept floors, cleaned bathrooms, and taught the inmates reading and writing.

"Why do you come here on Tuesdays and Thursdays?" I asked.

He laughed deeply, a laugh that came from the soul.

"I come in here to say hello to my good friend Willie—you know, the man who's always doing magic tricks for the kids."

Since I worked there, I knew Willie quite well; every day he'd come up to the cash register and pull pennies or one-inch washers out of my ears. I think everybody in town knew Willie.

"I've been trying to get that ole heathen friend of mine to come to church with me for nearly thirty years," said Mr. Moreland. "He hasn't taken me up on my offer just yet. But I think he will."

A few years later, when I was home from college, I ran into Janice at the supermarket. She and I reminisced for a few minutes about our days at Masten's—the woman was bitter, but deep down had a good soul—and then she said, "Do you remember that old man Mr. Moreland, you know the one who stunk to high heaven?" she asked. "He died a couple of months ago."

"Gosh, he just died?" I asked. "How old was he?"

"Ninety-two! And do you know, I went to the old man's funeral?"

"You did? Were you feeling all right?" I asked.

"Matthew, it changed my life," said Janice.

"Really?" I said.

"It was the longest funeral of my life, I think," Janice explained. "I bet you thirty or more people got up and said something about him. And the place was packed; I bet you there were more than five hundred people at that church. The most moving thing for me was the six former inmates who stood up and said that Mr. Moreland was one of the reasons they were on the straight and narrow. I sat there and cried the whole way through. I sat there thinking to myself, 'I know if I were to die that I would have a good number of people at my funeral, but would anybody be able to stand up and say that I changed their life?' That man changed people's lives! Person after person stood up and said that. And guess what else?"

"What?" I asked.

"He was worth more than one million dollars!"

"Are you kidding me? Why in the heck didn't someone buy that poor guy some deodorant?"

"I know," she laughed. "But yeah, he was worth a million dollars, and yet he lived in a twelve-hundred-square-foot shack for most of his life."

"His kids are pretty lucky then, eh?"

"That's just it; he didn't leave any of it to them. He gave 10 percent to his church, and the rest he gave to various charities."

"Wow, Janice, that's amazing!"

"Isn't it though? I want to be like him!"

"Well, you better not retire!"

"Ugh. I know!"

Though I know Mr. Moreland's life was hardly simple, he did

seem to inhabit the best parts of what it means to follow Jesus. He seemed to have life figured out. He made it seem simple. Perhaps this is just the nature of someone who follows Jesus for sixty or seventy years—rubbing up against culture and changing the world around them. But for some reason, I complicate it. It's no wonder I have such a difficult time just putting my left foot in and enjoying the dance. I'm learning that the people who dance are those who simply believe that God rarely makes a habit of hiding what he wants us to do. Most of the people I talked to about this book didn't think finding God's will was brain surgery. Sure, there are times when we are confused. I mean, most of us are confused a lot. But honestly, I think the "dancers" are correct; I'm not sure it takes all that much "searching" to figure out at least a little about what God desires from us while we're here on earth.

I mean, in addition to bits and pieces of his story being written down in Scripture and thousands of men and women throughout history giving us hints (and sometimes getting it wrong) about what he's all about, God seems to be constantly asking us to do one thing: Take the road less traveled, the hard path that only a few are willing to walk.

But missing that at times isn't entirely our fault. Unfortunately, over the years Christianity has been boiled down to only fragments of what Jesus taught. Today, it's more systematic theology and merchandising than it is a dangerous and provocative way to live life. No wonder so many of us are hindered by doubt, frustration, and fear. Instead of being truly curious about what life really is all about, we spend more time arguing about stuff that we won't find answers to this side of heaven. And the answers we do find, we don't always like.

I recently met a woman on an airplane who shared with me the secret to her own personal journey. "I want to envy the man who believes he knows truth so my appetite will always be whet with anticipation," she said to me, drinking Delta's finest wine out of a plastic cup. The woman was dressed in all black; she looked like she could have been from Manhattan, but was actually from Knoxville. "Matthew, I guess I am a believer in the idea that there's more joy in the searching than there is in the finding."

It's not like I don't see her point. I, too, enjoy the thrill of searching for God in my everyday story. I find a great deal of enjoyment in the actual search. But I also think that constantly living among the questions is odd and impractical, and quite frankly can lead to a very unhappy existence. I mean, why search if you don't plan on finding at least some of the answers once in a while? There's no need to find everything—that, I believe, is impossible—but I think if you're not at least hoping to find something on the journey, at least a little hope that surprises you on the journey, the search could end up bogging you down. And you don't want that.

Please don't think I'm suggesting that you should just settle. That's *not* what I'm suggesting at all. And I'm certainly not saying that you have to fall in line with the norms of evangelical culture—in fact, I hope you don't—I'm simply saying this: Make sure your spirit is willing to embrace and be content with an answer when you find one.

I know an awful lot of people who never stop searching. Some people die searching, still looking for that one light to guide them home or to someplace sunny and warm or, heck, maybe just New Jersey. Despite disagreeing with the lady I met on the airplane, I do know why she is so infatuated by the longing.

I think Tom Cruise might know why that lady enjoys the thrill of the chase. From the outside looking in, many might think that somebody like Tom has everything he would ever need—a job with celebrity, millions of dollars in a bank account, a beautiful wife, the ability to purchase any luxury his heart desires. And in addition to all of that, Tom's a brand name that wields power and influence. For better or worse, he's an American icon. But if you listen to what he says in interviews, Tom still very much has a longing for more, even if it is for things like speed, adventure, danger, control, or the next level. Sure, there are times when he seems to have found something that's meaningful to him. However, his actions within the media frenzy that surround him tell me that he still isn't satisfied—that having everything his heart desires isn't enough for him. He wants more. He needs another thrill. Now, whether he wants a bigger following or his own religion or just to squelch those rumors about him being gay, but whatever it is, he still seems to be looking for something. That's because I think there's a great amount of satisfaction in the hunt for meaning; for some of us, it can be like a drug.

If the truth were known, most of us just want a little security. The emotional kind. The spiritual kind. The physical kind. And how does security come about? Well, I think we learn these things by living. In other words when we live, we realize that God has a role for us in this story that he's writing here on earth. That's what life is all about, isn't it? To be a part of his story. To be certain that he is holding tightly to our personal narratives.

And this is what I've come to know: Even when I doubt, my unbelief doesn't mean that God isn't still there, holding me and guiding my story. And you know, sometimes that makes all the sense in the world and other times it feels like something from Aesop's Fables. For a long time I would have never known the kind of freedom to suggest that I go through times of unbelief. But I've learned that sometimes unbelief is a thread in my story of faith. It doesn't mean that my faith has disappeared.

This life we live is a journey. It's a journey that will have many seasons, some when I feel like I am close to God, others when I feel like I am dragging behind him, and still more when I have no clue where God is in my story. That's the story we read over and over again in Scripture, a rocky narrative that isn't perfect or ideal or magical. But it is a story about faith. The men and women curious enough to hold onto faith, eventually began to see what life's all about.

The hope in those stories—*God will be our foundation*—is somewhat similar to God's reminder to my friend Devon that he was God's art. I love the imagery of that phrase. For me, it potentially sheds a little light on what we find out about God in the first chapter of Genesis—the part where we learn that we are made in God's image.

I think Devon is right; we are God's art—a series of paintings that reflect his creativity. Art that tells his story over and over again, one that constantly reminds us of redemption, grace, love, freedom, and survival. If this is true, I want to be someone who enjoys God's artistic expression. I want to learn from each of the paintings that I encounter. I want to be someone who allows God the freedom to paint in me what he wants to reveal about himself, so others might possibly be able to learn something about him by looking at my story.

But I also know that my story will always be in process. There will always be something I don't understand. There will always be a part of this journey that I will have to leave in question. But I know this: I don't want to be that person who demands to be completely painted before I am willing to participate in the "hokey pokey." I want to dance. I want to do it the way God created me to do it. I want to have fun with it. I want to add my own color to it. I want to put my body in and shake it all about.

To a large degree, that's what life's all about.